THE CARSON HOUSE AND THE OLD FORT MOUNTAIN RAILROAD

THE CARSON HOUSE AND THE OLD FORT MOUNTAIN RAILROAD

A Stage Play and a Scripted Novella

FREDDY BRADBURN

freddysongs

CONTENTS

This book is dedicated to my wife, Susan Yergler Bradburn.

CHAPTER 1

John Carson Buys A Slave Who Really is a Princess

The Carson House

A Stage Play by Freddy Bradburn

Cast of Characters

John Carson-Owner of the Carson House and slave owner. Born in 1752 in Ireland.

Kadella-Slave bought by Carson. A former princess from West Africa. Purchased around 1798.

Young Sally-10-12 year old version of Sally Carson.

Sally Carson-Daughter of John Carson and Carson's deceased first wife, Rachel.

Young Davy-10-12 year old version of Davy.

Davy-son of Liam who is in charge of the stables at the Carson House.

Liam-Blacksmith in charge of the horses at the Carson House.

Lily Whitefeather-Wife of Liam, a full-blooded Cherokee.

Mary Moffett McDowell Carson-John Carson's second wife.

Eli-slave and friend to Kadella.

Samuel Price Carson-son of Mary Moffett and John Carson. Born in 1798.

Emma Trout-Mountain girl who falls in love with Samuel.

Emma's mother.

McEntire-Husband to Sally.

David Thoreau-Quaker minister who helps on the underground railroad.

Andrew Jackson-Friend to John Carson.

Davy Crockett-friend to John Carson.

Fatima-house slave at the Carson house.

An Auctioneer

Although based on actual history and some historical characters, this is primarily a work of fiction.

Part I

(Platform center stage-Kadella center stage on auction block. John Carson and small group of men bidding on her.)

John Carson
"I bid two hundred dollars."

Kadella (to audience)
That's the first words I hear from John Carson. Plum romantic ain't it? Me standing half naked on a platform. Looking him straight in the eye like I could stab him. Looking at him like the princess I was. Platform reminded me a little of my daddy's throne back in Africa.

My daddy was a king and I was his daughter. But a war broke out with another tribe over this or that. They was always fightin about something. But my daddy didn't know that the other tribe had sold out to the white man. These slave traders.

Bidder
I bid two hundred and twenty-five!

Kadella

My daddy got killed in the battle and I got captured and they put me on a ship like I was some kind of animal. Shipped me to Charleston and stuck me on the auction block. I didn't speak much English. Just the few words I'd learned on the boat. Old man helped me down in the hole of that boat. He teach me as much as he could. But he got sick and died and they threw him overboard right into the ocean. I's a young girl of 18, and I'd seen a few wars amongst our tribe, but I ain't never seen any cruelty compare with this. It was just getting started.

John
Two hundred and fifty dollars.

Kadella

When they threw that old man into the ocean without a prayer or a word on his soul--well, it made the soul of the world angry. My momma was a healer on the island and knew all sorts of herbs and potions and incantations and things, and she had taught me since I was a little girl. And living by the ocean, I learned a lot bout the soul of the world. Most white men don't know nothing bout the soul of the world. They got their Jesus, but he a pale rider to some of the deities I was acquainted with. And the white man don't seem to have any respect for things of the world. Always trying to tame it or subdue or make money out of it, or selling it, like they sellin us.

Bidder
I bid two hundred and seventy-five dollars.

Kadella

Human beings--treating us like their work animals. Those work animals more human than these white men. Anyway, I saw em roll quite a few dead people off that boat, and no wonder the way they had us crammed in there, and each time an albatross appeared and followed the boat. I knowed it was a sign. The poor soul of those dead people flying off, but not too far. Remembering, remembering.

John
I bid three hundred dollars.

Kadella
Man on the platform picking and prodding me. It was all I could do to keep from slapping his ugly old face. All these fat, slobbery white men were bout the ugliest things I'd ever laid eyes on. And speaking of eyes on, John Carson sure had his eyes on me. And he bought me for three hundred dollars. I figured that was a bargain for a princess, and while he was ugly, he wasn't as ugly as all those other loud, ugly, white men.

Auctioneer
Sold! To Mr. John Carson for three hundred dollars!

John Carson (*to audience*)
I knew I was going to bid on her as soon as she stepped up on the auction block. She was young, and beautiful and had a regal bearing about her. I would tell my wife that I bought her to help her in the house with the sewing and quilting. The way this slave glared at me when I bid. What was I getting into? This group was from West Africa. This girl was dark and her glare reminded me of the hateful Cherokee.

It is a strange sensation to buy another human. They are human, especially the women, but they aren't human like us. Three hundred dollars is a lot to spend, and I am frugal. That is why I treat my slaves well. It is not a system I particularly like because of all the trouble these slaves can cause. It is not like having a good horse or mule. I wish I could get the horses to do the work. I am fond of horses. But I treat my slaves well. It is an investment. The whole institution of slavery is rather odious, but it is the way things work. So be it.

Unchain her please. What's your name, girl?

Slave Trader
Her name, Kadella. She don't speak no English as far as we can tell.
Congratulations, Colonel Carson. You just bought yourself a princess.

John
A princess? I thought she didn't speak English.

Trader
She don't. They told us when we put her on the boat. Daddy was a
king. And just wait, she sure acts like a princess. Princess of slave ship.

John
Well, I bought a slave about five years back from the West Indies.
Fatima will teach her some English. "Kadella! Good you recognize your
own name. Come with me. I'm taking you to your new home. You're
mine now." (*Exit all but Kadella. She walks while speaking.*)

Kadella
And I rode in his wagon for three days. Each day took me farther
away from the ocean and into these dark hills. When we arrived, his
home was just a large log cabin with open fields near a river. It was
surrounded by dark hills and wilderness.

(*Enter Eli, Liam. Kadella and John.*)

John
Eli, this is Kadella. Take her to the slave quarters and give her to
Fatima. Tell Fatima to clean her up and then bring her to me at the barn.

Eli
Yes sir, Mr. Carson.

Liam

Got you a pretty one there, John. You got some jobs in mind for
her.

John

Claims she's a princess. Sure acts like it. Stared right through me the
whole trip. I understand she can sew, knit, and quilt and so she'll be
working with Fatima. She'll train her. She don't speak a word of
English yet.

Liam

Anything else in mind?

Carson

I hear what you're saying, Liam. My first wife dying so soon and me
marrying Mary Moffitt because she's the only woman of substance
around and her a widow too.

Liam

Not exactly a love match as we say in Ireland.

Carson

No but she's a devout woman who will give me a few more good
sons. And she's happy and busy with the house and her religion.

Liam

Yep. She's all the time praying with her Bible down on her knees,
but married to the likes of you, I reckon she'll need all the prayers she
can get.

Carson

Yes. That's the only time she'll get down on her knees. You know a man out here on the frontier has certain needs. Don't let Mary Moffitt see her yet. Mary being with our first child and us not married that long. Well, buying a young, light-skinned negress might not go over too well.

Liam

If you say so. I don't reckon Fatima is going to be all that pleased to see, what's her-name?

John
Kadella.

Liam

Kadella, the princess of the Carson House. Fatima might get jealous.

John

She'll be fine. She has no choice in the matter anyway. By the way, how the horses lining up? Today is Thursday, right? Lost track on the trip to Charleston and then the trip back. We're having the big race on Sunday.

Liam

Things looking good. Your horses ready. Ginger raring to go. Lily Whitefeather says the weather looks good. No rain.

John

How is it Lily can tell the weather four days out, and always be right?

Liam

Well, she's Cherokee and it's just built into them--to her anyway. Built into the generations, I guess. Like the Irish and whiskey. Speaking of which, we got a new batch aging and you're getting ready to tap into the Belfast batch.

John

Irish eyes will be shining. Good to be home. Better go up and say hello to the missus, then I'll come down and deal with Fatima and Kadella.

Liam

I'll put the horses up. I'm taking my boy, Davy, fishing at the river later. Taking your daughter too. Regular Tomboy that girl. (*Carson exits*)

CHAPTER 2

Sally and Davy Meet Kadella

(Fatima, Sally, Kadella, Davy. Music playing in the background.)

Fatima
That party going strong now. Now they want us out of sight,
especially Kadella here. Don't want them to start a bunch a gossip bout
a pretty new slave Mr. Carson just bought, but she a good worker I can
already tell.

Sally
My name, Sally, Sal-ley, and this is Davy, Da-vy.

Kadella
Sal-ly. Da-vy. I speak some English, but sometimes it's better to
pretend I don't. My name Kadella.

Fatima
We help you learn. Sally gonna help teach you. She can talk up a
blue streak.

Davy
Ain't that the truth. Sally knows how to talk.

Fatima
Kadella made her scarf here. Isn't it beautiful?

Davy
She really a princess?

Fatima
That's what Mr. Carson claims so we gonna play that up as much as we can. I think Mr. Carson likes the idea since he all the time drinking and gambling. It'll make a good conversation topic for him. He's always talkin up what he's got that others don't.

Davy
Where she from?

Fatima
Africa.

Sally
That's a continent.

Davy
I know that. I ain't completely ignorant.

Sally
You did not. I seen that look on your face. I seen that look in our little school plenty of times. When you were there, and not off fishing somewhere.

Davy
You're just jealous cause you have to go to school and I don't. . .
Listen, I hear my daddy's fiddle starting. The dance is starting. Let's go
watch awhile.

Sally
Yes. They get a little whiskey in em and it ain't exactly dancing. It
kinda genteel up at the house but when they outside those frontier
men start buck dancing. Well, it don't resemble any dancing I ever seen.

Fatima
You just be careful and don't get seen by anybody. I'm supposed to
be putting you to bed here soon.

Sally
Ah don't worry. Momma will be in bed with her Bible and earplugs.
She wouldn't be caught dead anywhere near the drinking and partying,
and she being pregnant, she tires out real early.

Davy
Come on. They got the bonfire going. They starting to jump
around. The sight of that would scare off any respectable Cherokee.

Fatima
Speaking of. How's your momma doing? I don't see her much.

Davy
Well, she don't get out much. She got her own garden and spices
and Cherokee things. She love papa but she misses her people. Talks
about wanting to go back. Have papa work for himself nearer the
nation. She ain't too keen on Mr. Carson, and ol Andrew Jackson
came down to the cabin today looking for papa. She despises Jackson.

Sally

Well, you just discourage such talk as that. You can't be leaving me.
Who'd I fish with and make fun of. Anyway you don't want to leave
Pleasant Gardens.

Davy

Pleasant who? What's that? Pleasant Gardens?

Sally

That's the name Mary Moffitt brought with her. Carson let her
re-name the place. Small sacrifice for all the other stuff he gets away
with. Gentleman farmer marries genteel well-connected neighbor with
the McDowell pedigree.

Davy
Pedi what?

Sally

Pedigree. Her name. The McDowell name. You must of been absent
from school that day too.

Davy

Prob'ly. Pleasant Gardens? Sounds like a cemetery to me. So come
on, Sally quit a-yammering. The fiddle and the whiskey and the
dancing, well, they be raising the dead.

Sally

Father always scheming. That's the politician in him. He's off to
Raleigh next week, not that I ever talk to him. Come on, I'll race you.
(*they run off.*)

CHAPTER 3

Drunk Andrew Jackson

Sally, Davy, Andrew Jackson.

Sally
Davy, when we going over to see the new slave? I can't wait for you
to see her.

Davy
You know they busy right now preparing for the dance and the big
ta-do tonight. We'll wait until the dance starts and everybody's occu-
pied dancing and getting drunk.

Sally
Yeah. I reckon. You gonna fiddle any with your daddy tonight?

Davy
Nah. I ain't good enough yet, but he teaching me. I can play
"Turkey in the Straw" tolerable well. But everything else sounds like
two cats mating.

Sally

Yeah, I heard you the other day. I'd say more like nine cats mating. Two doesn't give that racket justice.

Davy

You're funny, Sally. . . Oh no. Look who's stumbling down the path. If it isn't the honorable scalawag, Andrew Jackson.

Jackson (*a little tipsy*)

Hey young'uns, what have we here? Conspiring on some great adventure, I suppose.

Sally

I suppose not. I suppose you're here to lose more horse races.

Jackson

I remember you. You're Carson's youngest. You ride pretty well too, for a girl. I've got some of your father's excellent whiskey. I'm looking for Liam so he can look over my pony for tomorrow. Who's your friend here?

Sally

This is Davy. He's Liam's son. I darest say he could out ride you.

Jackson

Don't be impertinent child. Where's your father then, laddie? I need another drink with a good Irishman who knows his horses.

Davy

He's down at the stables. That's a Cherokee pony you got there. What's you do, steal it?

Jackson
Devil tongued young'uns. Be glad I'm in a charitable mood today.
How'ja know it's a Cherokee pony?

Davy
My momma is full blood. She knows her horses too.

Jackson
Then you're a little half breed then aren't you.

Sally
Pardon us, sir. We don't like that term round here. Matter of fact,
Liam might just whip your scrawny ass for insulting his wife that way.

Davy
My Cherokee momma could whip his scrawny ass.

Jackson
Be glad I'm in a good mood angelic children or I might. . .

Sally
What? Challenge us to a duel?

Jackson
Wash your mouth out with soap. But I'll leave that up to Carson,
who has killed a few Indians in his time, but never you mind. I will take
my whiskey and pony now to the stables and bid you a fond adieu.

CHAPTER 4

I Always Catch More Fish Than You

Enter Davy, Liam, Sally with fishing poles.

Davy
Where are we fishing today, father?

Liam
Where Buck Creek flows into the Catawba. So come on and don't tarry. There might be trout for dinner, laddie, and don't let Sally catch more than you, right Sally?

Sally
Yessir, Mr. Liam. I always catch more than Davy.

Davy
You do not.

Sally
Do so. How many did you catch when we went yesterday?

Davy

I don't know, that was a long time ago. Five or six.

Sally

You caught four and I caught six. It's like our birthdays. I will always be older than you. I'm eleven and you're ten.

Davy

Next month I'll be eleven too, so we'll be the same age.

Liam

Argued like a real Irishman's son. Now stop your prattle, we are here and you don't want to scare the fish away arguing about how many fish you're going to catch. You two together put Blarney Castle to shame. Now bait your hooks and have at it. I'm going on up the river a bit.

(*Liam exits*)

Sally

We been sitting here half an hour and nary a bite. Oh wait! I got a bite. Got it. Look at that Davy, a big brown. That's a nice one, ain't it.

Davy

It's alright, I reckon. Nothing special.

Sally

You're just jealous. Don't be jealous, Davy. You're teaching me how to ride. You're an expert horseman for a ten year old.

Davy

Almost eleven year old, and just be quiet. I think I'm getting a nibble.

Sally

Oh look. I'm getting another bite. Got it. Look at that. A rainbow trout. Look! What a beauty. Your father's going to like this one.

Davy

You stole my fish. That was the one nibbling at my line.

Sally

Go on, Davy. It's okay. You'll catch something in a minute.

Davy

A cold, probably. I wish the sun would come out. How's your new momma doing?

Sally

Can't say. Don't see her much. She's pregnant, and she's ornery when she's not pregnant. Don't like me much, I reckon. Thinks I'm unlady like and don't like me spending time with the common help and the slaves.

Davy

Like me and Fatima.

Sally

Yeah, but that's okay cause I don't give her no never mind and anyway she's got her nose in the Bible all the time. Where is Fatima? Not like her to miss the fishing.

Davy

Father says the Colonel bought a new slave. A young girl who don't speak no English. Fatima with her showing her around and such. Father says she claims she is a princess, or was a princess. Now she a slave. Says she from Africa, maybe the same place Fatima from. I don't know. Kinda anxious to see her. Father says she right purty.

Sally
Well, if father bought her I reckon she be. Remember when we saw my father and Fatima down here by the river. Father told us he was going fishing, but we followed him cause fishing wasn't something he did very often. . . Wait, I'm getting another bite. Got it. Ah another brown. . . Anyway, what we saw them doing wasn't fishing. That's three I caught. How many you caught, Davy? You eleven yet?

Davy
Cut it out, Sally. Quit teasing. I'm having a bad day. You got me all distracted.

Sally
After we finish fishing we'll go and find Fatima and see the new slave. You'll come with me won't you, Davy?

Davy
You sure you want to be seen with the common folk?

Sally
I'm sure.

Liam
What you young'uns talking bout? Hey, somebody did pretty good.

Sally
Thank ye, Mr. Liam. Two browns and a rainbow.

Liam

I caught a couple upstream there. Lily Whitefeather will cook them
up tonight. Sorry, son. Don't look like you did so good. What
happened?

Davy

My worm quit on me, and he was too ugly, and my worm looked
like Andrew Jackson. Nothing going to bite that.

Sally

Is Jackson coming to the race on Sunday?

Liam

Well, of course he is, after all the money he lost last time. He'll be
here. Maybe that'll put him in a bad temper?

Sally

He's always in a bad temper.

Liam

Well, never mind children. I have to go up and groom the horses.
Davy, you come with me. Miss Sally, if you wouldn't mind, go over to
my cabin and take our catch and help Lily clean those fish.

Sally

Yessir. Anything to keep me out of my own house. Speaking of a
bad temper, with Mary Moffitt with child, she's raging all over the
house. Fatima can't do anything right and now father has brought this
slave that Fatima's going to have to teach. I can't wait to see the new
slave. What's her name? You say she's a princess? Davy, you and me can
go see her later.

Liam

Here, slow down child. Her name Kadella and you leave Fatima alone unless you're willing to help. Carson says Kadella don't know any English. Maybe you can help her learn. You're good at a lot of things Sally, but talking is certainly one of your main strengths.

Davy
Ain't that the truth.

Sally
Spoken like a true Irishman.

CHAPTER 5

Sally Starts a Diary

Scene 6: *Sally, Fatima, gathered around Mary's bed. Sally is off to the side of the stage and reads from her diary.)*

Sally's diary: January 22, 1798

I'm starting this here diary that my brother gave me. He's a doctor, and it was a Christmas present. He helped me to learn to read and write along with Mrs. Greenlee who is a teacher who comes here a couple times a week. I was very eager to learn. Father isn't around much, and doesn't much care if I learn to read or write or not. He's too busy, and he thinks women were just created to be married off and make babies. Speaking of babies, Mary Moffitt is finally getting ready to have hers. Maybe it'll calm her down some. The midwife, Fatima, and Kadella upstairs with her right now. I'm going up when I finish this and watch. I ain't never seen a baby born before.

Fatima

It's a boy, Mrs. Carson! Look at that shock of black hair. What a handsome boy. Here, Mrs. Carson, you hold him, then I'll get him cleaned up and bring him back to you. What's you gonna name him?

Mary

Samuel, Samuel Price Carson. The Colonel and me decided on that if he was a boy, and the Colonel was convinced he was going to be a boy.

Fatima

Kadella, put some more wood on the fire. We don't want the baby catching a chill. This is the coldest January I can remember. You okay, Kadella? You look a little puny.

Kadella

Yes'um.

Mary

I knew it was going to be a boy, too. Do you understand me, Kadella?

Kadella

Yes'em. Sally a real good teacher. Your baby is a boy.

Mary

Well, I knew. I could tell. This my sixth child and I'm just turning thirty. I also knew cause I had a dream last night. I was asleep and Lord Byron came into the room.

Fatima

Who, Mrs. Carson?

Mary

Lord Byron. He's an English poet. He has a book called, "Childe Harold's Pilgrimage." He came in here last night as I was sleeping and he kissed me.

Fatima
I like those kind of dreams, Mrs. Carson.

Mary
Well yes, but that's not the point, but look at this black hair on this newborn baby. Lord Byron has beautiful black hair. Check the child's foot.

Fatima
Why, mam?

Mary
Byron had a club foot.

Fatima
His foot looks fine, mam. Here let me take him and clean him up. You need some rest. Come on, Kadella. You can help me. (*they exit with the baby.*)

CHAPTER 6

Andrew Jackson

(Outside. A table with a bottle of whiskey and two glasses.)

Enter Carson and Andrew Jackson.

John Carson

Well. well, well, look what the cat dragged in. If it ain't master Andrew Jackson. All 140 pounds of lanky swagger come to honor us with his equestrian skills. How many Cherokee did you kill on your way over?

Jackson

Well, look who it is. John Carson, the no good son of a bitch who cheated me out of a hundred dollars a couple months ago. It's a good thing I like your whiskey. At least you're good at one thing besides cheating an honest man out of his money.

Carson

How's life on the Tennessee Supreme Court? That august institution on this side of hell.

Jackson

Might more exciting than the legislature. That job bored me to tears. Bunch a shite eaters blabbing on and on.

Carson

Yeah, I imagine stealing Indian land a little more satisfying than making up laws that allow you to steal Indian land and then hanging 'em.

Jackson

Oh, the little joys in life. And it's land speculation, John. you know that. You an indian fighter like me. The savages don't understand the purpose of good land or the concepts of ownership.

Carson

Well, I'll drink to that. You can't even make a good slave out of them. Now let's try this malt whiskey. Been kegged for awhile now. Aroma of good ol' Belfast. I see you got a different ride this year.

Jackson

Speaking of Indians, got the pony from a village we raided. Cherokee pony. Leave anything you got in the dust and I got some money to win back on this trip.

Carson

We'll see. Here's to the Irish, Jackson. Slainte. . . Here, I'll leave the bottle with you. I've got to go up to the house and greet a few of the early arrivals for the dance tonight. Fulfill my official duties before I do some serious drinking. Mary Moffitt been on the warpath lately, so to speak. She's three month gone with our first child and is only in a good mood when she's sleeping. She hates the horse racing, but enjoys the hobnobbing with the local gentry.

Jackson
Your stable man, Liam, around? I wanted him to look over Lightning over there. We had a pretty long ride over from Tennessee yesterday, and I can share some of this malt with him.

Carson
Your horse named Lightning, huh? Only lightning gonna strike
around here is gonna be striking twice because of the money you're
going to lose tomorrow, but yeah, he's down at the stable. Don't get
him drunk before the dance now.

Jackson
He's one mean fiddle player too. Plays better drunk, I'd say.

Carson
Yeah, but he tends to speed up and I don't want some of these old
codgers passing out on the dance floor too early. Now I'll leave you
with that. In an hour or so, get your things, and come on up to the
house. Mary Moffitt is like everybody else. She don't like you but she
likes your title, Judge Jackson.

Jackson
Does have a nice ring to it. (*exits. Enter Sally and Davy with fishing
poles. They sit.*)

CHAPTER 7

Kadella Learns English and John Carson Pays a Visit

(Sally and Kadella. Sally reads from her diary.)

Sally

I saw my first baby delivered and now it's not been three months and Mary Moffitt is pregnant again. I can't say it is something I'm looking forward to myself. How that baby with blues eyes and black hair came out of Mrs. Mary, I don't know. Poor thing. That was her sixth baby and her not thirty yet, and now she's got another one coming, and after seeing what she went through and old John Carson not even here. Kadella, do you understand what I'm reading to you?

Kadella

Mostly, I do. I saw many babies born. My mother help dribble them into the world.

Sally

"Deliver," Kadella, the word is deliver not dribble, but you're learning to speak pretty darn good. Better than some of these people who were born here, and I'm beginning to like writing in this diary.

Kadella

You're a good teacher, Sally, and the people who come on Sunday to teach us the Bible. I don't understand much, but I listen. Why did your Jesus get nailed to a cross?

Sally

Well, I don't rightly know. To save us, I think.

Kadella

From who?

Sally

Ourselves, probably.

Kadella

Was he a slave, like me?

Sally

No.

Kadella

And Eli talks to me some when he not off in the field. He play the banjo and we sing some. Singing help me to learn your language.

Sally

Yeah, Eli is a good'un.

Kadella

I like it when you read to me from your dairy, Sally. It helps me learn. I like to listen to you.

Sally

Thank ye, Kadella. But the word is diary not dairy. A dairy has cows. A diary has words.

Kadella
Cows, and pigs, and hoses.

Sally
Right. But it's pronounced horses. But you're learnin real quick,
even though I don't talk proper. I better skedaddle. I'll get a whuppin
if I'm caught in your room this late, and father is back from the
legislature.

Kadella
A ske--daddle?

Sally
You know, go, leave. And whuppin.

Kadella
I know what a whuppin is.

Sally
Yes. I suppose you do.

Kadella
Sally. I need to tell you. I'm with child.

Sally
With child? You mean pregnant? Although it's not right to use that
word in mixed company.

Kadella
Why?

Sally

I don't know. It's like a curse word, I guess. I think men just make things up though. I know all about it though. I've seen it done. Twice. At the river. From a distance, so maybe I'm not an expert. Who is the father?

Kadella

Mr. Carson.

Sally

Father? Well, I shouldn't be surprised. . . Listen, someone's coming down the stairs.

Kadella

It's Mr. Carson. Run, quick!

Sally

I can't. The stairs are the only way out. I'll hide, where? In the little closet here. Try to get rid of him. (*Sally hides in the closet.*)

John Carson

It'll be good to be back at Pleasant Gardens. If I had to hear one more long-winded legislative speech from some bag-a-bones. Get back to my whiskey and the Christmas party, and sweet Kadella, beautiful and exotic, and the bonus of her not being able to speak much English. That kind of quiet is always a plus in a woman. I'll pull the carriage around to the barn and grab a drink of malt with Liam and pay her a little visit. It'll just be dark, and Mary will be asleep since she just had a child. (*Enter Carson*)

Kadella

Hello. Mr. Carson. You had a good trip, no?

Carson

Listen at you smooth talker. Your English has improved, even since
the three weeks I've been gone. Now enough chatter, I don't have
much time before I'm due up the house. My sons are coming in for a
visit. Take off your clothes. That's pretty plain spoken.

Kadella

Mr. Carson. I have been sick. Fatima says I'm with child and should
not do that anymore until. . .

Carson

God damnit. I thought we were careful. I must be the most fertile
man in the country. I just look at Mary and she gets pregnant, and
that's as it should be, but not you. And Fatima is wrong. Now we can
do it for a few months without any fear of you getting pregnant.

Kadella
No, don't, please!

Carson

Don't you resist! And don't raise your voice. You're mine and you'll
do what you're told. Princess or not.

CHAPTER 8

Fish Lips and the Accident

Sally's Diary: December 29, 1801.

Here's my history of Mary Moffitt McDowell Carson.
January 22, 1798. It's a boy.
December 19,1799. It's a girl.
December 6, 1801. It's a boy.

Three children in less than three years, and father not the least bit attentive. He's gone most of the time. The state legislature, his land speculation, his horses, his gambling. And me, thirteen years old and I've seen life, and birth, and death, and people fornicating, all in the span of a couple months.

Davy
It's bout time you got here. Fish ain't gonna wait all day.

Sally
Fish will wait fer me fore they'd bite your line, and I just got a lot on my mind lately.

Davy
Thinking too much. That's what school will do to you.

Sally
It ain't that. Kadella's little baby born, and it white as me, whiter
than you cause of your Cherokee blood.

Davy
That mean Mr. Carson the daddy.

Sally
Yep.

Davy
How you know that fer sure?

Sally
Let's just say I got some inside information. But I worry they take
the baby away, especially if Mary Moffitt sees it. Be a scandal, I reckon.

Davy
It ain't the first baby your father has sired out a wedlock, I suspect,
but he ain't a cruel man. He just a businessman. But he is a rounder.
He's out riding with my papa right now, over on the new tract, down
river.

Sally
Won't be the last either. Still don't make it right.

Davy
I reckon not. But a man's a man, I guess. I'm just glad my pa ain't
like that. Does his work, plays his music, and takes care of mama, and
mama takes care of him. I want to be like that.

Sally

Yeah, me too. A little cabin somewhere with lots of flowers and music. I sure ain't going to be having babies every year like Mary Moffitt. Poor Fatima and Kadella run ragged taking care of those babies.

Davy

You think fish have lips?

Sally

Do I think what? Do I think you have fish lips? No, you have a fish brain as is clear by that question you just asked me. But your lips are quite handsome.

Davy

You think I'm handsome?

Sally

I said your lips. I wasn't covering the rest of you, but yeah, you kind of handsome like ol Davy Crockett when he comes round. You think I have fish lips? Is that why you brought it up?

Davy

No, Sally. You have nice lips. Any fish would be mighty proud to have your lips.

Sally

You sure know how to sweet talk a gal, don't you?

Davy

You purty, Sally. If you were a fish, I'd kiss you right now.

Sally

I think you should drop all the fish comparisons right now. I ain't a fish and I sure don't want to be caught on a hook like some women are. But I might consider lettin you kiss me. I imagine you know how to kiss since you been practicing on fish; that is, when you can catch one. I hope you end up catching gals better than you can catch fish.

Davy

If I have you, I won't be needin to fish fer no others. (*they kiss*)

Sally

That was a mighty nice kiss. I don't have anything to compare it to since I ain't kissed nobody before.

Davy

Me neither. Let's make a pact that we won't kiss nobody else, and when we get old enough we can get married and do what we want to do. Look, Sally, I caught a fish with the pole just settin on the ground while we were kissing. Must be a sign.

Sally

I make a solemn promise on this fish to grow up and marry you, Davy.

Davy

And I make a solemn promise on this fish, that I caught, to marry you, Sally.

Fatima

Davy, Davy! Come quick! Your father has had an accident! He got thrown off his horse! He's up at the barn. They've sent for the doctor. Come quick!

CHAPTER 9

Six Years Goes By and the Wedding

Part II

(Six years later. Sally's wedding day. Mary, Kadella, much scurrying about. Adult Sally enters and reads a letter that falls out of her diary that she is moving.)

Sally

Dear Sally,

I'm writing this letter to say good-bye to you. I'm not much on writing things down since I missed so much school. I need to say good-bye in this letter because I'm worse at saying good-bye face to face. I don't really have any words, and none of them seem right anyway, except, you were my very best friend, and I was going to marry you. I'm sorry we have to leave, but it has been decided and I have no say. I am going to live with the Cherokee now that daddy is dead.

I don't think we should all together give up the idea of getting married. Life is stranger than fish lips. Well, that's about all the words I have. I will miss you. Tell Kadella and Fatima good-bye for me. Good-bye, Sally.

Sally (*doing her hair with Kadella helping.*)

"Good-bye, Sally." It's funny. I still have the crinkled letter that Davy wrote me years and worlds ago. I had not thought of him in ages, and here on my wedding day the letter falls out of my diary. Matter of fact, I haven't written too much in my diary in the last year. After Davy left things just changed for me. I didn't have anyone much to ride or fish with and slowly I just changed. I became more of the girl everyone else expected me to be. It just wasn't any use in fighting it. After Mary Moffitt had William last year, her fifth child with father, I started going to the camp meetings with her. I became fond of the singing and praying. Everyone was pleased, especially father. I'm 18 now and he thinks I'm practically an old maid. Since I'm the youngest of his children from my mother, God rest her soul, he's anxious to get me married off.

Kadella

Poor child is getting married today, but she isn't really a child anymore. Eighteen and a woman. A pretty woman. Here's the scarf I made for your wedding. Here, try it on.

Sally

Oh it's beautiful, Kadella. You're my very best friend. You were about my age when you came here.

Kadella

Yes, child. Got my own little cabin now Mr. Carson built out of guilt, I reckon. Seems like a long time, but this is your day, your wedding day.

Sally

Kadella you're the only one who understands. I don't know what to feel. I suppose I'm resigned to the situation and God will guide me, but it feels like I'm being sold off like a piece of property. Here I am marrying a man I danced with twice and talked to once, but father scoffs at the notion of love. He says it's up to the woman to make the home, and have babies, and love and obey their husband. It's in the Bible, he said, not that he would know much of the Bible. He said marriage is a contract and obligation, "Just look at mother and me." I wasn't sure how to take that, but I didn't really expect much else from father. He sings McIntire's praises, but that's just because McIntire hunts and drinks whiskey with him.

Kadella

In this world you don't stop sinning, you just learn how to hide it or ignore it like Mrs. Mary. Everything I've ever had they've taken away from me, but not my music, or my mind, or my heart. I have a good man on the plantation. Eli is a wonderful man, and we sing and play together when we can, and I love him. Mr. Carson is all into politics and is gone most of the time these days. Eli and I have to keep our love secret. "If Mr. Carson finds out," Eli says, he'll send him off. Off to work in his gold mine. I ain't working in no gold mine. I would have to run away," he said.

Mary
Would you two stop gabbing. Kadella get Sally dressed. She's due
downstairs in twenty minutes.

Kadella
Yes Mam.

Mary
Where is Sam? You didn't give him the ring yet did you? That boy
got his head in the clouds. He'll lose it in a heartbeat.

Sally
No. I think McIntire has it.

Mary
Oh Lord. He's probably off to the barn with father having a drink
of whiskey.

Kadella
There, Sally. You look beautiful. Now get downstairs fore Mary
Moffitt has a heart attack.

(*Enter Eli*)

Eli
Hey Kadella. You know I'm sick of all this. I'm thinking bout running away.

Kadella
"Run away. Where would you run away?"

Eli
Kadella, It's a big wide world. They places and they people who
help. I'd have to get up north. I've heard people talking.

Kadella
But they'll kill you if they catch you. I know that.

Eli
Nah, they wouldn't kill me. They'd beat me somethin awful, but
I'm young and strong and they have too much money in me. They'd
kill me in a heartbeat, but they don't want to kill the money.

Kadella
Well, we'll just have to be careful to keep our secret. I love you and I
don't want to lose you.

Eli

Maybe you run away with me. You know the camp meetings that Mrs. Mary keeps having, well, they a few preachers who preach against slavery, and there's people who are strong against it. I've been watching and listening just in case.

Kadella

We shouldn't be talking bout this. We just keep this secret.

Eli

Yes, but you know Mr. Carson bought five more slaves down in Charleston last September. Some of them mighty jealous of you and me cause they think we get special privileges. We just need to lay low a bit with Mr. Carson here for Sally's wedding.

(*Enter Mary and Sally*)

Mary

It was a lovely little wedding and wasn't Samuel the cutest little ring bearer. My own little Lord Byron, and Matilda, the flower girl, only eight years old and little William. Will you be going with McIntire soon?

Sally

Yes mam. Right after the dinner.

Mary

May God bless your new home with love and many children. You'll make a lovely mother just like you made a beautiful bride. Now I'm going downstairs. Kadella will help you with your things.

Kadella

Well, seems I'm losing another piece of me. Sure gonna miss you, child. You've been my very best friend here.

Sally

Oh Kadella. I love you so. I'm so scared. I don't want to leave and I hardly know this man. He seems so distant and sadly, he seems a lot like father. And I've never. . . never. . you know, done that. I'm scared.

Kadella

Well, honey, I'm not the one to help you on that subject. But I can tell you this much. You are smarter than he is, and that's all you have. He is your husband now and that will give him all the power over you, so you have to be smarter and survive. He will own you like me, but you can runaway if you have to. You"ll figure it out. Now don't be sad.

CHAPTER 10

Samuel Carson, Eli the Slave, and the Quaker

(Eli, Sam and, David Thoreau)

Eli

Mr. Sam, how old are you now?

Sam

I'm ten years old. . . Do I own you, Eli?

Eli

Well, Mr. Sam, by law, I'm considered property of your father, Mr. John Carson, so, but if you think about it no one should own anybody else.

Sam

Does Mr. McIntire own Sally? I heard her talking to momma that McIntire had beat her, and that he didn't own her, and she might run away. But momma said she couldn't on count that she was McIntire's wife, and he owned her, and she had to do better and not disobey her husband.

Eli

Mr. Sam, you a smart child and you seem to hear and take in about
everything round here. Ten years old and with the voice of an angel.
You going to be a good man when you grow up.

Sam

Like papa?

Eli

Well, you'll be a good man, but different. You already thinking bout
things I don't think Mr. Carson thinks about. You've talked to me
more in these five minutes than Mr. Carson ever did.

Sam

Is Sally a slave?

Eli

Well, no. The law is a funny thing. Everybody tell you you got a
follow the law and talk about justice and such, and then there's God's
law, but the Bible got a lot a double talk in it, so powerful white men
make the laws and then they tell you what the Bible is saying and the
Bible might be really saying something different, and sometimes the
law isn't really fair.

Sam

Momma says the Bible right all the time. It's the word of God and
we sing his praises. We having a camp meeting starting tomorrow. Lots
a singing and people from all around.

Eli

Your momma is a good woman, and I ain't speaking against the
Bible. But you'll understand when you get older. I don't know the
Bible as well as your momma, but I know people ought be treated
fairly. Let me ask you this? Am I a horse? Or a chair?

Sam
Don't be silly, No.

Eli
Law says I'm your papa's property. A piece of property. That makes
me the same as a horse or a chair and he can do anything he wants with
me cause he owns me, but he a fair businessman and he sometimes
treats me like a man. So am I a horse or a man?

Sam
I thought you were a chair?

Eli
Sorry. Here I am bending your ten year old ear with stuff I don't
even understand. But it means he could sell me off to somewhere and I
wouldn't have any say in the matter.

David
Eli, there you are. I been looking for you. I wanted to show you this
banjo I made. I modeled it on the one you made. Who is this handsome
little man?

Eli
This here is Sam. He owns the place, don't you Sam? Horses and
chairs. . . He's Mr. Carson's boy. Mrs. Mary will introduce you. She
proud of him, and wait til you hear him sing. This here is Mr. David.
He's one of the preachers come for the camp meeting tomorrow. He
gonna be staying in the spare room at the house.

David
It's a pleasure to meet you, Sam. I'm from Salem. Few days' ride east
of here. How old are you?

Sam
I'm ten, sir. Can I see your banjo?

Eli
You'll see it tomorrow, Mr. Sam. You need to run back up to the
house fore your momma start looking for you. She running round like
a chicken with its head cut off getting ready for tomorrow.

Sam
Yes'um. Nice meeting you, mister. I'll hear your preaching tomorrow.

David
Yes sir, Sam.

Eli
That's mighty nice wood work on your banjer. It play mighty nice
too. I'm glad you came back. You didn't preach last time. I didn't know
if you'd get invited back. Preachers that get to friendly with us slaves
sometimes get disinvited.

David
No, I think the music helped. Mary Moffitt likes me cause she
considers me an intellectual, I think, which negates my radical views on
slavery. I've explained that being a Quaker, I have christian ideals and
biblical interpretations that might clash with current views. I thought
this might get me disinvited. Quakers are often disinvited to most
things. And the fervor of this current religious uprising is a little
troubling to me. Intellectual it is not. Did you read the pamphlet I gave
you?

Eli
Yes sir. I did.

David
And then did you burn it and leave no trace of it or speak about it
to anyone?

Eli
Yes sir, and that's why I wanted to speak to you. Mr. Carson done
bought his way into the gold mining east of here, and the rumor is he's
going to move some of us off the plantation to work in his gold mine. I
ain't working in his gold mine.

David
Yes sir. This here is a nice banjo. . . (*quietly*) Well, we established a
station in Salem to help runaways, but we're just getting started. I'm
scouting things out with these preaching trips. This is about as far west
as I go, but I have a contact northwest of Asheville. I'll be back around
here in the fall. We can talk then, but don't breathe a word of this to
anyone.

Eli
No sir. I won't.

CHAPTER 11

Married Life

Sally

I listen to Kadella's words about being smarter than him. It's true, but the fence post outside his house is smarter than he is too. And he's mean. He reminds me of father except a lot meaner. Thinks he owns everything, especially me. Being smarter right now is not much comfort. He has carried me into his house. A fine house but not as fine as father's. It sits in a field in the settlement of Old Fort, not far from Fort Davidson. It is encroaching on Cherokee land and McIntire, like my father, fancies himself quite an Indian fighter. That's how they met. Killing Indians, drinking whiskey, and smoking cigars. That was the extent of our conversation on the hours-long ride over. Nothing more romantic than to hear about skinning, and gutting a hog. We arrived in his buggy right at sundown. He is outback gathering wood for the fireplace. I'm writing this quickly trying to delay the inevitable. I've decided to try the defiant, independent girl as my first strategy. My reputation precedes me.

McIntire

I got a nice fire going. Can you cook?

Sally

No, sir. My mother died and Mary Moffitt was too busy having young'uns.

McIntire

Well, I'll get my slave woman to show you. You'll learn quick. Now what you got your clothes still on for, girl? Hit's our wedding night. I'm going to see how wild you really are. So strip.

Sally

No, sir. I won't. . . I never done that before, and I'm afraid of you. We never even kissed.

McIntire

P'shaw. Kissing ain't nothing. I heard you a wild one. Fishing and riding with the men. Defying your father. Well, let's get this straight right now. I don't put up with no sass. You my wife now and you'll obey me, or I'll beat the wild out of you. I'm a hunter and farmer and a plain spoken man who needs a few sons, and you're gonna give them to me. Now strip or I'll come over there and do it myself.

Sally

I used to be wild, but I ain't wild no more. I'm a lady, and you can't treat me that-a-way. If you lay a hand on me, I'll tell my father.

McIntire

Ha! That's a good one. John Carson begged me to take you off his hands. You being 18 and not married. He said I could do whatever I wanted to with you. We're hunting buddies, ain't nothing closer than that. You mine now. (*Chases her off stage.*)

CHAPTER 12

Sally Meets Edgar the Bear

Dear Diary--May, 1808.

Well, so much for being smarter. The defiant wife got me a good black eye and a beating with a belt. I fought back, but that only made it worse. I prayed I wouldn't get pregnant.

I fell into a routine. McIntire would be gone, or working his farm all day. I began to enjoy writing in this diary and reading. I fancied myself as Jane Austen and was beginning to write and speak as if I was in an English novel, and I dreamed of someone coming to rescue me, but knew I had to rescue myself. But living in a dream world was the one thing helping me to survive. When McIntire would stumble in at night, and have his way with me, I would fantasize. (*McIntire enters with the head of a pig. Goes over to Sally grunting.*)

McIntire: (grunt, grunt!)

Me: (*thinking*) Maybe I skin him with his hunting knife, and mount his head above the fire place. McIntire was an amateur taxidermist, so there were stuffed and semi-stuffed animals all throughout the house.

McIntire: Oh, oh, grunt, grunt!

Me: Maybe shoot him and then stab him, and let the hogs eat him.

McIntire: Grunt, ohhhhhhh!

Me: Maybe pour boiling water over his head. Scoop his eyes out with a spoon, and feed them to the crows.

McIntire: "Snore, snore."

****

Sally

Dear Mr. Poe,

I enjoyed reading your story, "Pit and the Pendulum." It has given me some new ideas about how to kill my worthless husband, and I do aspire to be a writer like you someday, although I know it is not allowed for women to publish books. I write in my diary every day now, and I think you might appreciate my circumstances, maybe even write my story.

McIntire

Sally, Sally, get me a drink! Bring it to me out on the porch!

Sally

My husband is a hunter and taxidermist and so our house is filled with a bear, a panther, raccoon, and a goat, for some reason, all immortalized in their death stares. Since my husband is rarely here and seldom sober, I've given them all names and talk to them during the day. The bear is the first thing you see when you open the door. He is about six feet tall and looks menacingly as one enters the house. I named the bear, Edgar, after you. Edgar is going to help me kill my husband.

McIntire

Sally, Sally girl, did you hear me?

Sally

My husband is trying to get me pregnant, but so far he has been unsuccessful. He blames me, and his behavior has become more erratic, and now he beats me more often, and I just can't take it anymore. Please excuse my writing for I am practicing writing like you and I am improving my vocabulary. I really think he knows it is his fault that I am not pregnant. Something in his sperm perhaps (please pardon the impropriety). He recently bought several goats and slaughtered one, hence the stuffed goat, Satyr, in our bedroom. I've read a few things on fertility lately. Of course, I think it is poetic justice that such a scoundrel as him cannot bear any offspring.

McIntire
Sally! What are you doing in there! Bring me my drink!

Sally
I have it all planned out and will kill him when he comes in tonight. He will be drunk, so when he stumbles in, I will be holding his rifle behind Edgar the bear, so it will look like Edgar is holding the gun. When he stops in surprise, I will shoot him through the heart. That is kind of inspired way to kill someone isn't it? I have you to thank, Mr. Poe. But how to destroy the body?

McIntire
Don't make me come in there! Sally, you hear me!

Sally
My husband has publicly reprimanded me on several occasions at social gatherings. Once in front of many guests, he shouted he would burn our house down if I tried to leave him. Also, people know he drinks and smokes cigars, so after I've shot him, I'll lay him in his bed and douse the room with kerosene and burn the house down with him in it. I think this is clever, as well, since it will give him a preview of where he is going. Then, I'll ride distraught to my father's house and say my husband came home drunk, and fell asleep in the bed while smoking his cigar and caught the house on fire, and I was just barely able to escape by climbing out the window. Alas, my husband wasn't able to escape.

McIntire

All right, if I have to come in there. You gonna regret it.

Sally

"No, you gonna regret it."

There, is that not clever. No one will really suspect foul play, so if you decide to use the story say it was entirely invented. That is why I will not use my real name here.

Regards from your fan. *(Puts gun in the stuffed bear, and stands behind it.)*

McIntire

I'm coming in, Sally. Fetch me something to eat and pour me a whiskey. I aim to have my way with you soon. Here I come. What's this? My bear, I killed with my bare hands. Pointing my gun at me! What's this? I told Carson that last batch of whiskey was bad. Blam! *(shoots McIntire. He falls.)*

Sally

Good shot, Sally. Right in his shriveled up, stingy little heart. Thank you, Edgar, you're a true friend for ridding me of this sorry man, and now I am free. Now I wish you could help me drag this bastard to the bed. Oh, never mind, I'll just douse the room with this kerosene. Take a log from the fire and this place will burn to the ground. Sorry about that Edgar and stuffed friends. You will be set free to go to the spirit world as you must burn up with him. Poof. *(exits, re-enters with John Carson.)*

Sally

Oh father, it was awful. McIntire came in drunk and the last thing I remember he was lying in our bed smoking a cigar. I fell asleep and the next thing I remember, I woke up choking and the smoke was so thick,

I couldn't see. I dropped down to the floor, and called for my husband but he didn't respond, so I crawled to the window and was able to crawl out and fall to the ground. In a moment, the whole house was engulfed in flames. My poor husband didn't make it. He perished in the fire, and I lost everything.

Carson

How are the goats? Are the goats okay?

Sally

The goats? Yes. I suppose. They were outside. The livestock is fine, and my horse, since I rode here.

Carson

Good. Poor McIntire. And the body?

Sally

Burned to a crisp.

Carson

Well, I'll take care of the arrangements, but God Dammit! He owed me money. Devil's got him now, I suppose. You'll want to stay here for a while, but we're letting rooms now so you'll be taking up a room. Maybe I'll send you to my son's plantation on Green River. I don't really want a widow old maid daughter here indefinitely.

Sally

Oh father, you're too kind.

Carson

I ain't been home a week and already everything's going to shite. Don't talk to me. You causing me enough problems. You come running back here after your husband gets burned to a crisp. You probably drove him to it, and you not giving him any children, and why you started talking all proper all of a sudden? Couldn't be McIntire. He only knew about fifty words and most of those were curse words.

Sally

I've been reading. Taking books from Mary's library. There's one called "Pride and Prejudice" I just finished. I want to be a writer too.

Carson

You're already a worthless female. You don't need to add writer to your list of worthless endeavors.

Sally

You are too kind, father.

Carson

No, I'm one of a kind and now I'm going to go check on my whiskey and try to gather some sanity back.

Sally

Eli, I'm going to go look at Fatima's old room. I so miss her, but if I move in there for a while, I won't take one of father's precious rooms that he rents.

CHAPTER 13

Ten Years After, John Carson Loses His Mind, and Kadella's News

Part III

Sally's Diary

June 24, 1818

Well, ten years have gone by and I'm still here living in Fatima's old room. My father is still gone much of the time. Politics and gold mining, and the usual slew of vices and now he's up in his 60's, so he's lost a step or two. When he's here, he mostly ignores me or confuses me with a servant since I live in the servant's quarters. I also tend father's herd of dwindling goats. I think father has given up on the business of goat testicles as a medical advancement since they stopped working for him, I suppose. I am now 27 and an old maid quite content in my spinsterhood, and I am writing novels.

Mary Moffitt

Morning, father. Sit down and have some breakfast. Don't forget to have Eli gather chairs and clean the field for the camp meeting on Sunday.

Sally

I told you, mother. We are having high tea in the English garden. I'm researching for my new novel.

Carson

We're having high what? And who are you again? I will take care of it, mother, but we have the dance on Saturday, so there is much to be done. The Devil on Saturday night and then God comes limping in with a hangover on Sunday morning. I know how he feels.

Mary

Please don't talk that way, and you don't know how it feels because you never went to church on Sunday, although you did limp and whine.

Carson

How are my goats doing, my servant? Mary, why is a servant eating at our table?

Mary

That isn't a servant, John. That is your daughter, Sally. I know you're losing your mind, but really? The price of so many hangovers.

Carson

Sally. That isn't Sally. Sally died in a fire years ago.

Sally

No, father. I'm right here.

Carson
Poor Sally.

Sally
And the goats, what's left of them are fine. They miss you.

Carson
What goats? Who said anything about goats?

Mary
Oh for heaven's sakes, John. Never mind, just eat your breakfast. Kadella! Come here. Go get Eli and have him look after the Colonel about all the arrangements. . . Now Sally, hasn't Samuel turned into the most handsome of young men? Lord Byron would be proud.

Sally
Yes, and he is my model for my next novel.

Sam
Please don't talk to me like I'm not here.

Sally
You meet a mysterious stranger who captivates you. (*a goat baa's*).

Sam
Well, the satyrs over there seem to like it. High tea with the goats. If you'll excuse me, I'm going for a walk.

Mary
And I have a thousand things to do. Come on, Sally you can help me. (*they exit.*)

(*Enter Kadella and Eli*)

Eli

Hey there, Princess Kadella. How is my baby doing this morning?

Kadella

Your baby?

Eli

Yeah, you know. My sugar, my sweetie, my darling.

Kadella

Oh. Fine. Mrs. Mary wants you to come up to the house and take care of Mr. Carson and all the arrangements for the weekend.

Eli

You mean the dirty work. His sons doing all that for him now, especially Logan, which is good since ol' Mr. Carson ain't right in his head anymore. How you doing? You look a little tired.

Kadella

Well, might as well tell you now as later. Speaking of babies, I think I'm going to be having one. I'm going to have your baby, Eli.

Eli

Well, knock me over with a banjo! You shore?

Kadella

Eli. . . Yes, I'm shore, and before you ask. Yes, It is your child. Mr. Carson ain't paid me a visit in over a year, but we still gotta be careful cause he forgets and he mighty possessive and jealous, and now he crazy too, so it best he don't know.

Eli

You right bout that. Glory be, A baby, A baby. Ain't that somethin. That baby need to be born free though.

Kadella

Eli, don't be gettin any wild notions just yet. If we be careful, and play it right, we be okay. Sam likes us and everybody likes Sam, and he twenty now, and the oldest son.

Eli

Yeah, Sam be our best chance probably, but we have to celebrate. I'll come over to your cabin after dark. Everybody be either running round getting ready for the big shindig or tuckered out by working on it.

Kadella

I love you, Eli. Now I'm going down to the barn, and gather up some eggs, and do my morning work. You need to skedaddle up to Mr. Carson. (*he exits. Kadella gathers basket and walks.*)

CHAPTER 14

The Return of the Native

Kadella

Get outa my way, rooster, or I'll ring your neck. I got to gather up these eggs. You leave these hens alone, strutting around like Mr. Carson himself.

Davy (*grownup Davy appears, Kadella doesn't see him at first. He speaks.*)
I reckon a rooster got a right to crow.

Kadella

Lord-a-mercy! Everybody going crazy here. Now roosters talking back to me. Oh wait, it somebody. Step outa that shadow, mister, and kindly tell me what you doing in the hen house.

Davy

Counting my chickens, I reckon. It been a long time, Kadella. Catching any fish lately? Sally still round here somewhere?

Kadella

Well, I declare. I recognize that mischief in your eyes now, but that beard covers the rest of your face. What you doing here?

Davy

Oh just passing through, I left the nation when my momma passed away. Been a traveling man ever since. Learned up on the fiddle right good, so I heard there was a big ta-do here tonight, so I made a little detour. Ain't much changed. Old Mr. Carson cantankerous as ever? Sally married with a bunch of young'uns?

Kadella

Mr. Carson got old and bout lost his mind. The rest of time he cantankerous, but sometimes just crazy with delusions. He won't admit it though, so we have to kind a work around it. You right. Not much changed in the twenty years you been gone.

Davy
How bout Sally?

Kadella
Oh yeah. Seems you did ask bout Sally. Now there's a story.

Davy
And?

Kadella
I gotta get these eggs back up to the house. I tell you later.

Davy
Kadella, don't be funnin with me. Tell me.

Kadella

Well, Sally got married to old man McIntire, but a few years back he burned up in a fire and Sally came back here. They ain't no young'uns. Mr. Carson thinks she's dead, because she's living down in Fatima's old room who died a long time ago. She's a lot different. Proper young,

well, not so young, woman. She been reading a lot of books and
writing some of her own.

Davy
Well diggity dog! That is some story. She going to be at the dance
tonight?
Kadella
Don't know, but I reckon I could do some coaxing.

Davy
I'd like to surprise her.

Kadella
She'll be surprised all right.

Davy
It okay if I bunk down here in the barn tonight?

Kadella
I reckon, just don't let Mr. Carson catch ya. Now I gotta get back
up to the house. Sure nice to see ya, Davy.

Davy
You too, Kadella. You too.

CHAPTER 15

Sam Wrestles a Wildcat

Mary

Sam, stand up straight! How am I going to get this shirt finished
fore the camp meeting if you don't stand up straight? Lord have mercy!

Sam

You mean so Kadella can finish it. Momma, I'm almost 20 years old
now. You gotta stop treating me like a baby.

Mary

But you are my baby, Sam. You gonna sing at the camp meeting,
and shine and love the Lord, and be saved in the blood.

Sam

I love the Lord but some of those preachers shouting and hollering
and speaking in tongues gets on my nerves.

Mary

Now, Sam, all those preachers ordained and sanctified. That
Quaker fellow you like gonna be there. He's a little too abolitionist for
me, but he's smart and educated, and interesting to talk to.

Sam

Good, I can have someone to talk to at least. David, David Thoreau is his name. Now let me go. I'm going for a walk up Buck Creek. I won't be back until near dinner.

Mary

Don't be late. Don't fall asleep. You been acting funny lately. Remember what happened to Rip Van Winkle.

Sam

I won't. Maybe I'll meet a mysterious stranger like in Sally's new book.
(Sam exits and then re-enters and sits by a creek and begins to write a letter.)

Sam *(reads aloud)*

June 24, 1818

Dear Step-Brother,

I'm sitting up past the fishing hole you showed me on Buck Creek. It was your favorite fishing spot when we were kids. I hope this finds you well. I have walked these four miles because I am trying to clear my head. My mother dotes after me something awful and father is grooming me to be a politician like him, but I am nothing like him, but it seems my path has been chosen for me. Mother is having one of her camp meetings tomorrow, and I'm losing interest in all the hollering and "hell and doom" talk. I hope there's a few pretty girls there to flirt with.

Anyway, I hate to trouble you, but I thought you might could offer me some advice or solace at least, perhaps I can pay you a visit at Green River soon. . .

Sam

Hey ho! Is there somebody there? There, in the brush behind the sycamore. Tell me you're not a bear or a panther, or a highwayman, because I'm getting ready to lower my aim with this pistol I carry.

Emma

I ain't no bear, and I ain't no panther, I ain't no highwayman, but my momma says I'm part wildcat and part deer. What you doin way up here?

Sam

Uh, I'm Samuel Carson. I just walked up here to be alone with my thoughts. Won't you come out from behind that tree? Or? Now where did you go? You were there a second ago. Maybe everyone's going crazy? (*she jumps on him from behind.*) Oh, what! Get off of me! Stop you're choking me! You're hurting me!

Emma

You give, mister? You give? You done messed with a wildcat. I might just claw your eyes out and put'em in my soup. Say uncle, say uncle!

Sam

Uncle! uncle! Don't kill me! I give! I give! I'm sorry. Are you Cherokee? Please let me go. I'll give you a dollar? Okay, Thanks.

Emma

I can wrestle a panther. You ain't much of a wrestler are you? You a dandy? A gentleman up here with your fancy name and your fancy pistol. And nah, I ain't no Cherokee. Just a wild mountain gal bout to kick your lily white ass. Sure, I'll take a dollar, and maybe that fancy pistol too.

Sam

Well, that's quite an introduction. You certainly have a way. Here's
the dollar, but I believe I'll be keeping my pistol. Might I ask who you
are since your handprints are on my throat?

Emma

Well, fancy boy. My name Emma. Emma Trout.

Sam

Like the fish?

Emma

Don't be fresh with that smart mouth of yours. I live way up on
that ridge, up there. Don't hurt your neck now. I live with my momma.
She raised me, but so did all the critters here. I can run fast as a deer,
can jump like a cat, and wrestle like a bear. What can you do?

Sam

Well, I'm a good singer. I fish a little bit. I'm a pretty good orator. . .

Emma

Please stop right there. You're boring everyone to death. That tree
over there falling asleep. Don't flinch. I ain't gonna hurt you. Your
words are fancy and boring but your mouth shore is pretty. I think I'm
going to kiss it. Close your eyes (*they kiss*). . . That was nice. You ever
kissed anybody like that?

Sam

Well, no. Not ever like that.

Emma

No, keep your eyes closed and count to three. Very slowly. It's
witching time.

Sam

One... Two... Three... Hey, where did you go? Emma... Emma Trout... She's disappeared. What just happened here?

CHAPTER 16

The English Novel Goes South and David Thoreau

(*Sam enters.*)

Sally, you ready? Dance going to be starting soon.

Sally
I'm only going to gather material for my novel, so remember, this is an English estate and you're Lord Byron.

Sam
I wonder if anyone tells Lord Byron that he looks like Samuel Carson.

Sally
Maybe I'll meet a handsome stranger.

Sam
Well, ol Dan Tucker will be there. If you can get past the buckskin, and chewing tobacco, and a few missing teeth, he might do.

Sally

Sadly, Lord Byron you just described most of the eligible bachelors attending tonight.

Sam

I'm glad we put the goats up. . . Oh, Mr. David Thoreau will be there. He's here to preach for the camp meeting on Sunday.

Sally

Ah! The seductive gentleman Quaker, but he is an educated man which sets him apart here. That's why Mary Moffitt tolerates his abolitionist views.

Sam

Yes, at least I'll have him to talk to. I doubt there will be any eligible ladies here tonight. What would Lord Byron do?

Sally

Lord Byron married his cousin, a mathematician. He called her the princess of parallelograms, and come to think of it. You're only my half brother.

Sam

You must really stop reading Poe.

Sally

Although, my book will never be published. I would hate to see it censored and cause a scandal, although, that would make it widely popular, and then ultimately published, and then banned. I will put Mr. Thoreau on my dance card. *(they exit.)*

Enter David Thoreau and Eli)

David

Hello, Eli. you wanted to talk to me. Here, I'll pretend to be showing you my banjo. Are you playing with the band tonight?

Eli

Yes sir, and I did want to talk. I'm ready to run. Kadella is pregnant with my baby and I gotta be a free man. Kadella not due for about six months. By then, I can be in Ohio, and then we can get Kadella and my baby out. I memorized the stars like you told me. I'm strong and I know the mountain trails round here from the hunting Mr. Carson done.

David

Oh hold on. Let me think. I can get you to the safe place beyond Asheville. It's a difficult journey.

Eli

I know it is. But Mr. Carson acting crazy and no telling what he might do. People saying he's gonna send a bunch of us away to work in the gold mine once the crop is in.

David

Let me think about it. . . Here comes someone with a fiddle case. You know who this is?

Eli

Kadella said he's a half-Cherokee fellow who lived here as a child. His daddy took care of the horses, but he got himself killed, and the boy and the momma moved away.

Davy

Howdy, fellers. Somebody told me you might need a fiddle player fer the dance tonight. My name's Davy, they call me Gypsy Davy.

David
Well, it's a pleasure to meet you, Davy. Sure, a dance can always use
another fiddle player.

Davy
I appreciate that.

Eli
We're just getting tuned up a little bit. You know the "Golden
Slippers?"

Davy
Yep. Let's give it a turn and get these revelers started. (*they play as
the scene ends.*)

CHAPTER 17

Fish Lips Again

Sam

Sally, do you hear? The music is starting. Let's go down and make an appearance. I don't want to stay long.

Sally

Well, let it settle in a little bit, then we'll make our appearance since we are family of the host.

Sam

Well, you know, it's going to be a little less formal than that. Father and his buddies been at the whiskey for awhile now. So will you take my arm and we can promenade as we walk from the grand house to the dance pavilion?

Sally

Thank you, Lord Byron. Such a gentleman, and only my half-brother.

Sam

Well, I'm sure I don't want to know what you mean by that. Oh, step lightly, watch out for the goat shite. Look, we are right on time.

The few gentlemen and ladies present are civilized, and father and his rabble are still with their whiskey by the barn. (*Enter David Thoreau.*)

Sally

Mr. Thoreau, how nice it is to see you again.

David

Miss Sally, you look radiant in that dress. May I have a dance?

Sally

Why, Mr. Thoreau, I'll have to check my dance card. Oh look, I have a space coming up next. Perhaps a waltz. I hear you have influence with the band.

David

Of course, Hey, Eli, you guys play a waltz? You know the "Tennessee Waltz," don't you?

Eli

Yes sir. Coming up.

Sam

I'll leave you two to dance and I will make my way to the food. Sally, it's a little tiring to pretend to be an English gentleman all the time. Being in your novels is exhausting.

Sally

Oh Sam, you are so droll.

David

What did he mean, Miss Sally? (*band begins to play.*)

Sally

Oh, Mr. Thoreau. Never you mind.

David
Milady.

Sally
You dance extremely well for a Quaker.

David
I think you mean that as a compliment.

Sally
Oh truly. My mother is fond of you. Your manners, your intelligence, but she is wary of your radical, abolitionist views, but I find them exciting. You're a handsome man, Mr. Thoreau, if I can be so forward, but as a writer, I must object to the word "Quaker." It reminds me more of some of these mountain creatures writhing in their fake ecstasies, and kissing poisonous snakes. I wonder, does a snake have lips? Oh I apologize I am talking too much.

David
Oh no, you're quite correct. People of my religion go by another term. You can simply call me "friend." And I assure I won't be kissing any snakes, lips or not. Although, I have met some women who could hold their own with poisonous snakes, but writhing in ecstasies could be another matter.

Sally
Why, Mr. Thoreau, friend. You will make me blush. Should we ask for another waltz?

David
Eli, boys in the band, may we request another waltz?

Eli
Yes sir. What will it be boys? We know a slow waltz?

Davy
Dear lady and sir, I have an original waltz I would humbly like to play fer you? It's called "Fish Lips?"

David
"Fish and chips," an apt title indeed.

Davy
Not fish and chips, sir. Fish lips.

David
Well, does an instrumental need to have a title? Now suddenly creature's lips have become a thing.

Sally
Well, play on, musician, whoever you are. (*They dance.*)

David
Thank you, Miss Sally, that was a wonderful dance. Perhaps I can request another before the night is through.

Sally
Yes. I will consult my dance card over by the drinks.

Davy
Let's take a break, boys. Carson and his crew are coming and they'll be no stopping when they get going.

Sally

We better move over, speaking of Quakers. The cloggers and the buck dancers are converging.

David

Miss Sally. I do so enjoy conversing with you. I have to go up to the house and consult with Mrs. Mary about the camp meeting tomorrow. I will return. Talking to you makes me feel as if I am in an English novel.

Sally

But you are, Mr. Thoreau, you are.

Davy

Excuse me, miss. I noticed you here, and wanted to ask you something while the band is taking a break.

Sally

Yes sir, you may, although I don't believe I have made your acquaintance. What is your question?

Davy

Does a fish have lips?

Sally

Is this an impertinence? Innuendo? A trick question, or a riddle?

Davy

A riddle, yes, and isn't it just like Sally to answer one question with four.

Sally

Who are you, sir? What is the riddle? You are keeping me in suspense.

Davy
Well, a hint, I have made your acquaintance, and asked you the very same question a long time ago. Look at my eyes and think of me without a beard.

Sally
On my! No! It can't be. Davy? Davy from my childhood when I roamed the river and woods in my romantic wildness.

Davy
The very same. Why are you talking that way?

Sally
Davy! How? I barely can remember you. I have changed. I have educated myself and become a lady. A lady of letters and a writer of novels.

Davy
Which letters? All or just some of them.

Sally
How droll. You were always the merry prankster, were you not? But what brings you here after all this time, all bearded and buck skinned up.

Davy
Well, I'm a traveling man now. Wandering minstrel, if you put me in your book. They call me Gypsy Davy. I play dances and other occasions where I can get food and board and a little money.

Sally
Sounds like a romantic life.

Davy
Only if you're reading bout it in a book. Bum, vagabond, petty thief, what's in a name, right? I believe I was at school that day.

Sally
But what brings you back here? Not many dances or occasions in this neck of the woods, and nothing but screaming wilderness beyond these courtly torches.

Davy
Let's cut to the chase, or should I say let's cut to the fox hunt. It's you. I came back here to see you. I was playing in Raleigh and who should I run into, but Mr. Carson. He didn't remember me until I mentioned my father and so he told me about the upcoming dance, and it made me think of you. I asked Kadella when I arrived and now here I am. I came here to see you.

Sally
I am left speechless, Davy.

Davy
That is a good sign, I think.

Sally
The collision of past and present befuddles me. Repels me. . .

Davy
I mean to take a bath.

Sally
But attracts me as well, and as far as my novel, you are dark, and perhaps handsome, but not tall. Not tall at all.

Davy
Well, two out of three is not bad. I am bunking in the barn tonight.
Maybe you could come for a visit after the dance. We can sit down by
the creek where we used to fish.

Sally
The lady of the house to come visit the stable boy. This is a plot
twist I did not expect.

Davy
Think about it. I have to get back to the band.

Sally
And I have to go up to the house. I have some notes to take. (*they
exit*)

CHAPTER 18

Talk of Escape

Kadella

I can hear the dance has ended. I didn't hear any shots, so no one got murdered. That must mean it was a success.

Eli

Down right, civilized. Miss Sally was there, and some of the ladies. Preacher David was there. It got wild after they left. The whiskey was flowing, but no fights to speak of. How are you feeling?

Kadella

Tolerable well. Why are you looking that way?

Eli

Kadella. I'm going to run. I'm going to escape. You're going to have our baby, and I want it to be born free. And the rumor is that Carson is going to send me to work in his gold mine since the crop is in, and I insulted his goats.

Kadella

Oh Eli. Don't. Think about this. If you get caught, they may kill you, and even if you make it, what then?

Eli

Don't worry, Kadella, Mr. David is going to help me. He has people
and stations all the way up to Ohio where I can stay. I have about six
months before the baby is born. I'll get established and then I'll get Mr.
Carson to give you your freedom, and you'll join me and our baby will
be born free.

Kadella

Mr. Carson ain't going to do that. Not in a million years.

Eli

Mr. David will help convince him. Anyway, Mr. Carson so crazy.
No tellin what he might do.

Kadella

Eli. Everything I've ever had in this world, either been stolen, lost, or
taken away. And I finally find somebody that gives me the greatest gift
of all and now you bout to leave. I just don't know if I can take it.

Eli

Miss Sally will help see you through it. I's got to do it. That's all
there is to it.

Kadella

Miss Sally livin in a make-believe world anymore. Maybe she take
me with her. Disappear into a book where people are happy. People get
lucky. That ain't me. When you going?

Eli

Few days. Mr. Carson will be gone again fer a week. Full moon will
be gone so the night sky will be dark. Come out on the porch, and I'll
show you the map of stars. Gonna follow the stars.

Kadella

They are right pretty. Makes you wonder why the world like it is with all this meanness.

Eli

It ain't all meanness. The stars make ya remember that they's a lot of good and beautiful. It just hard to see it sometime.

Kadella

Speaking of Miss Sally, ain't that her walking toward the barn. I'd know her step even in the dark.

Eli

I reckon it is. She was at the dance fer a while. Danced with Mr. David and she talked with that fiddle man who showed up.

Kadella

Hmm, that fiddle man used to live here when she was a little girl. They taught me how to fish, and Davy was good with the horses, his momma was Cherokee, but the daddy got killed and they moved away, and then he come back here after all this time. He's bunkin down at the barn.

Eli

I reckon she's paying him a visit. Maybe to talk about those childhood days.

Kadella

Maybe, or maybe somethin else. Miss Sally been alone a long time here writing those romance novels. Maybe she going to put herself in one.

Eli
Well see, there is some goodness in this world. Sometimes things happen cause they suppose to happen. People have some good luck that changes everything, or sometimes you have to give the good fortune a nudge.

Kadella
I hope you right, Eli. I hope you right.

CHAPTER 19

A New Chapter

Sally
Ho! Davy, you in there?

Davy
No, I'm over here. The night so pretty and peaceful. I was sitting out here hoping you might come. Stars sure are pretty.

Sally
Yeah, remember when we used to sit out after fishing all day or riding our ponies. What were we, ten? Seems like a lifetime ago.

Davy
Yeah, funny how things turn out.

Sally
Funny, been such a long time. I had just thought it never happened. I'd see us in a dream ever now and then, but it was more dream than memory. I became a different person and that childhood was someone else. Now you're here and all those memories and feelings came flooding back more real than when they happened, almost.

Davy

Yep. The first time I laid eyes on you after all these years, well, it hit me like a brick. Grown up woman, a lady, all beautiful and all, but in there was Sally, the little wild girl I knew. I had imagined you in my mind's eye for so long, so when I saw you there at the dance. I nearly keeled over.

Sally

I know now I've been making up stories and reading books, and I think I'm making it all up. Inventing places and situations that are foreign and exotic, but really you can't get away from your own real life. You're making up stories that somehow come out of your life, your own mind, your own heart. The stories are my life, just wrapped up in dreams, or stars, you know?

Davy

Well, some things don't change. You still talk just as much as you used to, only it's a lot more fancy and proper, and, what's the word, beautiful. And here I've been trying to touch your hand to hold it fer ten minutes now.

Sally

I remember now when you asked me if a fish had lips? What were we talking about?

Davy

Fish.

Sally

Are you sure? I think we were talking about lips? I've never kissed anyone with a beard?

Davy

Neither have I.

Sally
Matter of fact, I haven't kissed anyone in years, unless you count
kissing Sam on the cheek.

Davy
I kissed my horse once. Now there's some lips fer ya.

Sally
Now I'm jealous.

Davy
Don't be. She got me out of a real scrap one time. I owed her. But I
don't think she liked it. Maybe we should kiss and make it even. I
washed up after the dance. (*they kiss.*)

Sally
I can't believe this is happening. I must be in my book.

Davy
Yes, a new chapter.

CHAPTER 20

Camp Meeting

Mary Moffitt
Sam, are you ready? We need to get down to the field and make sure everything is ready for the camp meeting. The morning after a dance and the whole place is upside down.

Sam
I'm ready, mother. And I made sure I sent word to the slaves to get things ready, and I just came back from there while you were getting ready. I've been ready for an hour. The people are gathering, and it's a beautiful morning.

Mary
I'm almost ready. Come let me look at you. My, you are handsome. My own little twenty year old Lord Byron.

Sam
Lord Byron was a heretic mother. An atheist.

Mary
But a very charming and handsome atheist. Okay, I'm ready, let's go down. (*they join a small group in chairs. Sam sits beside Sally.*)

Preacher (*shouting*)
My friends, the great awakening is upon us. Satan is amongst us and we must cleanse the world and cleanse ourselves of sin, oh Lord! Oh Lord, smite the sinner and strike him down! The world of lust, and avarice and sin is like a great plague upon our land and it is up to us to bring righteousness back to the world. Oh smite the evil sinner. . .

Sally
(*whispering*) What does smite mean, anyway? These backwoods preachers are all the time smiting and striking things.

Sam
I think it means to hit someone really hard like with an ax handle or something.

Sally
If he smites one more thing, I'm going to scream.

Sam
Don't, they'll think you've been filled with the spirit. Good or bad. Exaltation or exorcism. The devil is amongst us.

Sally
I know I kissed him last night.

Sam
Does the devil fiddle?

Sally
Like the devil. Oh good, he is through smiting everything. It's time for you to sing. Go on. Sing pretty, it's the witchin hour.

Sam
(*singing*) I went down in the valley to pray.
Learning about the good old way.
And who would wear the starry crown.
Oh Lord, show me the way.
(*Everybody joins in*)

Sally
That was beautiful. I love it when everyone joins in singing like that.
Who is that? A new preacher? I wish David would speak. This looks
like another smiter if you ask me.

Preacher
My friends, before I begin I would like to introduce you to a young
girl from our little church on the mountain. We are a small congregation, but filled with love of the Lord. The little girl is going to sing fer
you all, and she has the voice of an angel. Her name is Emma Trout.

Sam
Emma Trout, did he just say Emma Trout?

Sally
That's what he said. Look, she certainly is pretty.

Sam
But I know an Emma Trout and that is not the Emma Trout I
know.

Sally
Where did you meet an Emma Trout?

Sam
Oh I went up Buck Creek halfway up the mountain to think about
my future, and I was sitting there minding my own business when this

wildcat of a girl jumped me and got me in a headlock and made me say uncle, and then she kissed me on the mouth.

Sally
Sam Carson, and you did not tell me this? What kind of half-brother are you?
(*Emma looks at Sam and sings the same verse he sang.*)

Sam
Shush! Listen. She does sing beautifully. My God! But it can't be the same person.

Sally
Well, I was wild once too, and how many Emma Trouts can there be. You'll just have to go talk to her after the preaching and find out for yourself.

Sam
Yes. Maybe I can suggest we sing something together. I think there is a break after this smiter. I'll approach her then.

Sally
Yes. I'm going over to talk to Mr. David Thoreau.

Sam
Excuse me. Are you Emma Trout?

Emma
Yes sir, Mr. Carson. One in the same. It's okay, I'm not going to bite you.

Sam
Well, if you're the Emma Trout I met up the mountain a week ago. Well, I'm not so sure.

Emma

Did I skeer ya, Mr. Samuel Carson? You seem more at home here
than scaling Rock Creek.

Sam

Well, I'm certainly not used to getting jumped on from behind by a
wildcat, or a mountain witch. Are you a mountain witch? Like now? A
shape shifter?

Emma

Whatcha talkin such stuff fer, and us at a camp meeting singing to
the Lord. I's just a poor mountain girl protecting her property. Oh, by
the way, you sing real nice.

Sam

You do too, and when your claws are retracted, you're almost pretty.
That's a nice dress you're wearing.

Emma

Why Mr. Carson, I bet you say that to all the gals. My momma
made it. It's the only one I got. These moccasins are the only shoes I
got. I don't like to wear shoes too regular cept in the wintertime.

Sam

What does your momma do?

Emma

She raises parcel of corn and beans. Soil thin and puny so high up
on the creek. We do some hunting. Turkey and squirrel. And we like to
eat'em raw. Oh, and ravens. We bite their heads off, and momma pretty
good at casting spells.

Sam
You like to go on with me, don't you? Do you ever talk serious?

Emma
If I talk serious then I have to think serious. Me and momma have a hard life since daddy died. Momma been sick and this is the first place we been in months and the first people we seen, cept when I saw you. I like you, can't ya tell? But I can't like ya too much cause you a rich man who shouldn't be giving me the time a day. So being a wildcat or a witch is a spell better than thinking yourself in a corner or a circle bout tomorrow and all the troubles just waiting there. How's that fer serious?

Sam
Let's sing a song together. Our voices don't know who is rich and who is poor.

Emma
You know "Fair and Tender Ladies." I just know the mountain ballads. Those are the songs my momma taught me, and the Bible songs.

"Come all you fair and tender ladies.
Be careful how you court young men.
They'll appear like the morning star.
They'll appear and then they're gone.
If I was a little sparrow,
and I had wings and I could fly.
I'd fly to my false true lover.
And he would pass me by.

Sam

That was beautiful. What would your ravens say?

Emma

The ravens would say be careful, Mr. Carson. Don't lose your head.

Sam

I'll visit you tomorrow, if that's okay. What time?

Emma

Why the witching hour, of course.

Davy Crockett and Andrew Jackson Advise Sam

(Sam, Davy Crockett, and Jackson)

Davy Crockett

Well, young Sam Carson, how the hell are you? And congratulations on your election to the state legislature. Now answer me this. How in the hell did you go get yourself involved in a duel when you ain't been a politician more'n a month? That must be some kind of record. Even Jackson here, who everybody despises, even his friends, didn't get challenged until three months. Anyway, your daddy brought us here to help since he told us you was a momma's boy and didn't know which end of a gun to hold.

Sam

Well, I appreciate the help but I'm a fair shot with a pistol. I just never got into hunting with a long gun.

Davy Crockett

Well, that will work in your favor a little. Now how in the world did ya get yourself in this scrape?

Sam

I had just started my campaign when my opponent, Vance, a doctor up in Asheville, insulted my father, and since I'm the one currently running for office I had to uphold the honor of the family.

Davy

Well, honor is not a word I'd use with your father. Skinflint, miser, drunk, fornicator, those words come to mind. Did he call your father any of those names?

Sam

No, he called him a traitor.

Davy

Well, them is fightin words. Why didn't you just whoop his ass right then and there. How big is he? You yourself is a bit puny.

Sam

Vance? Oh he's about four foot nine, and he has a hump-back.

Davy

Four foot nine, and you what five foot two?

Sam

Five foot three.

Davy
Well, ya should have just hauled off and beat his ass, instead
of all this duel nonsense. Although, a humpback. It might have
resembled midget wrestling. I used to enjoy midget wrestling at
the county fair. That's where I learned to wrestle alligators.
Anyway, that's why I brought Jackson along. I'm more expert
with killing bears with my bare hands. Bare hands, get it? And I
could break Jackson in half with one hand tied behind my
back, but Jackson has fought several duels and, surprisingly,
he's still alive. So I'm gonna let him tell his story now, although
whatever he tells you, you might want to consider the opposite.

Jackson
It was a dark, and stormy night in Wayman's Tavern. . .

Crockett
No, wait. The short version.

Jackson
Well, this feller I challenged was a crack shot, which I didn't
know at the time of the challenge. I knew he was a much better
shot than I was, so I came up with a plan that when we were
back to back and we took our ten paces, I would turn fast and
holler like I was going to shoot quick. I figured it might rush
him, and he'd shoot wild and miss, and then I'd shoot.

Sam
Seems like a reasonable plan. Did it work?

Jackson
Oh no, not at all. I did all that, but the scoundrel lowered
his pistol and shot me square in the chest. I felt the bullet go in
right near my heart. It knocked me back a few feet.

Crockett
Lucky fer Jackson here, he has a shriveled up little heart so
the bullet stuck.

Jackson
So I stood there a bit shaky, but I lowered my pistol and
shot him and killed him on the spot, and well, that bullet is still
there inside me.

Crockett
Jackson too ornery to die. Devil don't want him. He'd mess
up hell.

Sam
So I should let Vance shoot first?

Crockett
Oh hell no. What kind of shot is Vance?

Sam
I don't know. About the same as me, I've heard.

Crockett
Well, that's okay, but he being a humpback will give him an
advantage. He'll be a harder target to hit. What part of him you
gonna shoot at?

Sam
I don't rightly know. The chest?

Crockett

Maybe. Depends on how humped over he is. I'll be your second. Jackson has business elsewhere next week. When is the duel set?

Sam

In a week. Just over the border, in Saluda, since it's illegal here.

Crockett

Well, get yer pistol and let's do some target practice. Get ya up to snuff. One good thing is Vance is a doctor. If he shoots you, maybe then he can save you.

CHAPTER 22

Emma Trout

Emma

A duel? What is wrong with you so-called civilized people? Have a
little spat in some fancy ballroom, then you go out and point guns at
each other and try to kill each other. Then that starts a war, and then it
makes everybody else, mostly poor people like me, go out and try to kill
people bout like us we don't even know. You can have yer civilization
far as I'm concerned.

Sam

I'm sorry, Emma. You're right, I wish I could get out of it, but I'm
in politics now and I have no choice. It's the honorable thing to do.

Emma

Piece a paper honor. You could be doing something useful like
learning to race the deer or catching rabbits with your bare hands like
me. Or just staying up here and loving me.

Sam

That's very tempting. I love you. I wish things were different. I've
thought about it a thousand ways and try to change my mind every
time I lie down to sleep, but I can't. And now this duel. I might die.

Emma
Well, Sam, when it rains it pours. I wasn't gonna tell ya right off, but I'm gonna have yer baby. Yep, you ain't gonna challenge me to a duel are ya?

Sam
A baby?

Emma
Yeah. You know a person, only smaller, cries a lot, and it's no wonder coming into this crazy world.

Sam
A baby. Good Lord, maybe I should duel myself. That way I might die.

Emma
But one of you would live, and that's the one that's gonna be father to yer baby, but don't worry, you don't have to marry me. That is, if you live through the duel. I knew you couldn't ever marry me, but that's the price of being a wildcat, or a deer. If you just live in the moment, the moment can come back and bite ya.

Sam
I'll take care of you, Emma. I'm sorry. This is my fault. I'll take care of you and the baby.

Emma
Ain't yer fault, and me and the baby can take care of ourselves. You've got a duel to fight, you know, to protect your honor. Oh, and you're having a baby with a no count dirt poor mountain girl. You can't marry her cause, you know, you got to think of your honor.

Sam

But I still love you. I'm sorry. It's not like that. Maybe I should
marry you and we could run away.

Emma

You forgettin somethin. I never said I wanted to marry you.

Sam

My heavens! What am I doing? Just give me some time to think this
through. I want to do right by you.

Emma

I know you do. Time to stop talkin and start doing.

CHAPTER 23

The Duel

Crockett
Well, what a beautiful morning. It's a good day to die, right
Sam?

Sam
Don't say die, Davy.

Crockett
Well, it's a good day to live too. Did i tell ya? I'm going to
Texas next month. The Republic of Texas. If you live through
this, you oughta come down too. I got some pull in Washing-
ton. I'll get ya some soft appointment. Jackson has more pull
than me. Where are they? It's damn impolite to be late for your
own duel. Maybe he won't show.

Sam
He'll show. He's coming from up Asheville. Just takes a
little longer.

Crockett
Why duels have to be fought so early in the morning?

Sam
Tradition, I guess.

Crockett
Hang tradition. It's too blame early. I can see gettin up early
to kill a deer, or a panther, cause they early risers, but men
aren't, and he's doing it on purpose. Showing up late. Trying to
make you nervous.

Sam
Well, it's working.

Crockett
Now listen, Sam, just remember what I told ya. Turn at the
exact same time you say ten. Turn like you do when you're
doing one of those fancy dances, then steady yerself, lower the
pistol and shoot for the center of the chest. Don't go fer the
head, too easy to miss. Now you're a tender hearted fellow,
Sam, but remember, you have to be fierce, and have murder in
your heart. I was at a duel once where both combatants
chickened out, and pledged to walk their paces, and then turn
and shoot into the air. Now I advised my friend, who was one
of the duelists, to call off the whole thing. I asked what is the
point if you're just going to shoot in the air. He said it was an
honor thing. Well, they both paced it off and shot into the air,
and my friend happened to hit a turkey that was flying over and
it landed on him and killed him. So much fer honor.

Sam
What if I miss?

Crockett

You won't. You've had a good teacher. Me and Jackson. Jackson a scoundrel but he's a crack shot. But, if you did miss by some accident of fate, then you just have to stand there and hope he misses. This dueling is just crazy. Why rich men want to invent a way to kill each other when they have everything is beyond me. Course the rules are crazy too. No wonder poor people don't fight duels, besides the fact, that they have better sense. Another reason is by the time they've counted to ten, they'd be so far apart nobody'd get hit. That is if they can count to ten.

Sam

I hear a carriage. Here they come.

Vance

Good morning, gentleman. I regret this argument has come to this, but to preserve my honor, I am here. This is Buchanan. He is my second. Shall we proceed?

Sam

I regret this too, Vance, but this is your provocation and I stand before you to restore and preserve the honor of my family's good name. This is my second, Mr. David Crockett of Tennessee. I am ready.

Crockett

Okay, gentlemen. Show your pistols and stand back to back. When I drop my handkerchief, you will take ten paces and by my count, when I reach ten, you will then be free to turn and fire.

One. . . Two. . .Three... four...five...six...seven...eight...nine... Ten. Blam! *(Vance falls.)*

Sam

I did it! Davy, I did it! What have I done?

Crockett

You did. Look, you shot Vance right in the center of the chest.

Sam

Is he dead? I didn't want to kill him.

Crockett

He's not dead yet, but he will be. We miles from any help. You ain't a doctor are ya, Buchanan?

Buchanan

Nope. Wouldn't matter. Carson shot him right near the heart as far as I can tell. Fair and square duel though. Help me load him in the carriage.

Sam

I didn't want kill him. I didn't want to fight a duel in the first place. It's father's fault.

Crockett

Oh quit ya blubbering, Sam. It's done now. Ya did what ya had to do and ya did it well. It's a mean world out there. Killin' just a part of it. Birthin and dying and all that comes between it. Ya can run on back to that mountain gal ya been seein.' Funny, ain't it. It right honorable and correct to kill somebody, but layin' with a woman below yer station is downright forbidden. You rich people got it all wrong. Upside down world.

Sam
I didn't want to kill him.

Crockett
Well, that's what upholding the family name will do fer ya.
Now I'm going to ride on back ahead of ya, and deliver the
news. They'll be quite a bit of celebrating to do. You can take
yer time. Stop by and see yer gal. Then you can show up and be
the hero of the hour.

Sam
Don't want to be no hero.

Crockett
Comes with the territory I'm afraid. Nothing to be done.
You think about Texas now. Lots of opportunity there. It's
wide open. No mountain gals, but lots a purty senoritas. I'll
send word to Jackson. He'll be pleased and want to take all the
credit.

CHAPTER 24

Beginnings and Endings

(Sam and Emma's mother)

Sam
Hey there! Anybody home, Emma, Emma you in there?

Emma's mother
Emma ain't here. She gone.

Sam
She's gone? Where? Where did she go?

Emma
Other side of the mountain. Some of her daddy's family over there in Tennessee. She going over there to have that baby. She said to tell you good-bye, and she didn't want anything to do with you anymore.

Sam
But. I wanted to talk to her. I wanted to tell her that I'm going to Texas, but I'm coming back.

Mother

She knows you leavin'. She a foolish girl, but she not dumb. She
knows you leavin', and she knows you can't marry her.

Sam

But, I'm sorry. I do love her. I want to do right by her.

Mother

Those just words, Mr. Carson. Do right? What you mean do right?
There's only one way to do right and that's marry the girl. You rich
people kill me. You want to have it all. Come up here and knock up a
poor mountain girl, but, of course, you too good to marry her. She
good enough to lay down with but not good enough to marry.

Sam

Here. I have some money to give her. Can you make sure she gets it?
It's three hundred dollars.

Mother

She don't want yer filthy money. She gone where she can get a little
schooling and make her own way in the world. Then she raise her baby
the way she want to.

Sam

It's my baby too. I want to do right by them.

Mother

Then marry her. That is, if you can find her.

Sam

I can't. Here. I'm leaving the money here on this fence rail. It's
wrapped in this letter I wrote her. Please see that she gets it. That's all I
ask.

Mother
Words and paper. One's worthless and the other don't mean
nuthin...

Sam
I'm sorry for all that has happened. I will come back. I promise.

Mother
You won't be back. If I could take that roll a money right now and
bet it, my bet would be that you won't come back. (*they exit.*)
****

(*Enter Sally and Davy*)

Davy
Sally, I'm gettin an itch.

Sally
You probably got fleas from the goats.

Davy
Not that kinda itch, but them goats part of it. If I had charge of the
horses that'd be different, but I ain't no goat herder. Especially these
goats. They like little devils, and with Mr. Carson not needing them
any more. I'm just gettin' restless. Not many dances going on. I think
we oughta pack up and hit the road fer awhile. Let you see a bit of the
country.

Sally
Davy, I just can't leave.

Davy
Why not?

Sally
I don't know. I just can't. I've never left before.

Davy
Well, it's high time then, with Mary Moffitt in bad health and John Carson thinks you're dead, and Sam taken off to Texas. I'll fix up one of the old carriages. Hell, I'll put wheels on the ol' rickshaw, and we'll ride west to Knoxville, then Memphis, and down the Natchez Trace all the way to New Orleans. I know folks all the way down where we can stay, and there's dances. Make a little money. I've saved up a little goat money besides.

Sally
You haven't been selling goat elixir on the side have you?

Davy
Nah! Nothing like that. It'll give you new things to write about. A high flown lady like you seeing the world.

Sally
A distinguished lady robbed of her inheritance runs away with a common shepherd.

Davy
Don't call me that.

Sally
But no, Davy. It would cause too much of a scandal. We're already living unmarried and in sin, but at least, it's a secret.

Davy
Secret my arse. Pardon my french, milady. It ain't no secret and if it is, nobody round here cares. Would you please get yer life out of one of

yer novels fer ten seconds and think about how much living we could do.

Sally

I just can't up and run away with you. . . unless. . .

Davy

Unless what? Oh I see. I think I left somethin out. Pardon me, Lady Carson. You know, I was worried bout telling you this so I rehearsed what I was going to say a bunch of times. Even the goats got tired of hearing it, but dang-a-mighty if I didn't leave out one little part.

Sally

And what was that?

Davy

Let's see. Let me go back over it. I reach in my pocket fer somethin, then I go down on one knee, and I ask. Sally Anne Carson, will you marry me?

Sally

You pullin a prank on me, Davy? Remember what a hard time I used to give you when we were kids fishing. How I would catch more fish than you. Is this a way of getting back at me, but before you answer. Yes, I will marry you. Grand lady marries a . . .

Davy

Stable boy and they run away together. But just so you know, I don't want no big ta-do wedding. Just me and you and a preacher.

Sally

You're right. It'll be me and you against the world, and seeing the world. Seeing the world close up. Nothing between us and our true love ways. There's a camp meeting a week from tomorrow. I think Mr.

David Thoreau will be in attendance. He can marry us by the river. Down by the spot where we said good-bye to each other as kids.

Davy
There you go, putting me right back in your novel with you, but that's alright this time. It'll give me time to fix up the carriage.

Sally
And I want Kadella to be there. Kadella can play her thumb piano and sing something.

Davy
Yes, Kadella should be there. I love ya, gal. We going to have a good life. We starting out a little bit later than most. But that's a good thing, I reckon.

Sally
Let's go down to the creek and look at the place we'll be married. Come on. (*they exit.*)

(*enter Kadella and Eli*)

Kadella
You leavin' ain't ya, Eli. You don't have to say a word. I can see it in your face.

Eli
Yes, Kadella. I got to. Word is Mr. Carson sending us to his gold mine. I was running away anyway, but I'm leaving tonight as soon as it gets dark.

Kadella
You be careful, Eli, and you come back to me. You come back to me and our baby.

Eli

I'll come back, Kadella. I'll be back fore that baby is born. I'll be up north in three months and that'll give me three months to get you and the baby free. I'll come back and I'll be a free man.

Kadella

You just stand up right now and go. Don't you tell me goodbye. Everything I ever loved has left me. You just go and I'll say hello when you return. I love you, Eli.

Eli

I love you too, Kadella. I'll be back. (*He rises and exits.*)

The End of Book 1

CHAPTER 25

Old Friends Meet, Ben Leaves the War, and a Quaker in the Making

Book Two: The Old Fort Mountain Railroad

Sally–From Book 1, in old age.

Kadella–From Book 1, in old age.

Ben–Sally's son, deserts from Civil War.

Andrew Milton–Abolitionist minister who establishes station on underground railroad.

Ariella Isabella–Mexican orphan adopted by Andrew.

Joseph–son of Kadella, former slave who ran away.

Jimmy–convict brought to work on the railroad. Musician who helpd form a band from the group of convicts.

Beulah–female convict brought to work on the railroad. Sings with the band and becomes friends with Jimmy.

Bones–Convict brought to work on the railroad. Former slave who ran away with Joseph.

Starlight–Convict who likes to sit in trees and talk to the stars and planets.

Bertie–convict and Beulah's best friend and friend to Starlight.

Elizabeth–mountain woman courted by Ben and Joseph.

Sally and Kadella, July, 1863

Sally

How the time flies, dear Kadella. You have been my friend for most of my 72 years in this world. You taught me to take pride in myself, and stand up for myself. Killing my scoundrel of a first husband, for example. I couldn't have done that without you.

Kadella

My, my Sally. You're a sight fer sore eyes. Whatcha doing back here? I haven't laid eyes on you in years and years.

Sally

Come down from the mountain to see my brother. Bury the hatchet, I guess. Old John Carson would like that phrase, but I wanted to visit you most Kadella. How old we've become.

Kadella

Oh, child, You still a youngun compared to me. Some say I'm 94 years old. Course nobody knows. That's the trouble with living too long. Everybody that would know is dead and everybody that's alive don't much care. How's Joseph? How my boy doing up on your mountain?

Sally

He's doing fine. We don't see him much because the war is still going on. He's still hiding out down in the hollar. Andrew's looking out for him. I'm glad he decided to stay here instead of going to the north.

Kadella

Yes, Lordy, Lordy. Run away from slavery just like his daddy did, but at least I know where Joseph is and that he's safe. I hear you and Davy had a child, a son?

Sally

Yes. My,my, has it been that long? He's all right. Like a lot of boys he went off to the war. We tried to stop him but he is head strong.

Kadella

I wonder who he gets that from?

Sally

But he saw right a way. War isn't a game, so he ran away and made it back home a year or so ago. We are hiding him because they hang deserters sometimes, but we don't think anybody will come searching for him. There is the Boone family that lives about ten miles from us. Their father is at the war. We have to watch out for them because they've been known to turn in yankee sympathizers, but they are the exception. The few people we know and see are against the war.

Kadella

I hope the war ends soon and I can see Joseph one last time. I'm trying to finish this quilt but my eyes so bad now, and it gets so lonesome here. What happened to that sweet boy, Sam?

Sally

Oh poor Sam. You know, he moved to Texas, and became Secretary of State. He married and had a daughter, but he died of Tuberculosis in '38. I was familiar with that disease because of the Bronte sisters. My, my, 25 years ago. It's hard to believe.

Kadella
Who?

Sally

The Bronte sisters, oh never mind. They were writers.

Kadella

I remember that sweet, sweet boy. What happened to the mountain
gal, I can't remember her name? He shore was in love with her back
then.

Sally

Yes. It's peculiar. He did come back. But Emma had died, but the
child she had was a girl. She was living up on that mountain with her
old mother. Sam adopted her. Her name is Elizabeth and after Sam
died she moved back. She's living not far from us in her mother's old
place. She's turned out a lot like Sam--sweet and kind. She married a
mountain boy, but he died early in the war.

Kadella

Lordy, lord, all these memories of people come flooding back. Sally,
my child, you pouring these stories out like one of your books. You still
writing your stories, girl?

Sally

Not much anymore. I've said all I need to say. I'm about to write
the epilogue to my diary too. I'm giving it to Ben so he can read it after
Davy and I are gone. Ben's turned out to be a good fiddle player, maybe
better than Davy, but until this war is over no one is going to get to
hear him. But the word around here is that there was a big battle in a
place called Gettysburg and the rebels were beaten, and the confeder-
ates will lose this war eventually and slavery will be finished.

Kadella

I've seen the end of it out of these blind eyes, and a road climbing up to the sky, and a new world coming. I'm glad you come to see me, Sally. You were always the best one.

Sally

Bye, Kadella. No, no, you were the best.

CHAPTER 26

Andrew Speaks of Emerson and Ben Meets Stonewall Jackson

Ben

The first thing I remember when I came to was a dead body lying on top of me. I opened my eyes real slow and I lay real still. I could hear people talking and guns going off not too faraway, and it all begin to come back to me. We marched in a line across the field and I remember the strange sensation of bullets whizzing by like bees or something. The first man I saw shot was a young boy just in front of me. It made this sickly thud and it knocked him back into me, and I'll never forget the look on his face. I let him fall to the ground and suddenly some union boys charged us and you couldn't tell who was friend or foe. I must have got hit with the butt of a rifle because that's the last thing I remember until now.

Now it is quiet and the smoke and noise of battle has quieted down. I'm talking to myself right now just to make sure the world knows I'm still alive. I'm still alive, world, and I'm getting the hell out of here. I should have listened to my momma and daddy. Famous last words. One taste of this war is enough. I'm going home. So I'm pushing the body of this dead soldier off of me and gathering my thoughts. I gather better if I talk out loud.

Okay, if I head south, I'll pass through our lines and appear just to be one of the wounded. I have a pretty nice gash in my head, then I'll just keep walking. If I get caught as a deserter, I'm likely to get shot or hanged. If I stay, I'm likely to get killed in battle. But I am done with this war. I'll lay down this rifle, pick up this pistol, and just start walking. I've lived in the mountains all my life, my daddy was half Cherokee. I'll just have to travel by night and off the main roads and follow the stars south.

Andrew

The act of Congress is a law which every one of you will break on the earliest occasion—a law which no man can obey, or abet the obeying, without loss of self-respect and forfeiture of the name of gentleman.

Ralph Waldo Emerson

I had a different life. I wasn't born a mountain preacher. I was born into a well-to-do Boston family and I attended Harvard Seminary School. How did I end up here? I've always lived a double life. Eventually, I used it to my, and runaway slaves, advantage. In 1858, I was twenty years old and living in Concord, Massachusetts. I was often a guest at Waldo and Lydia Emerson's home. They both, but especially, Lydia, was outspoken about the abolition of slavery. Waldo was more reserved but just as passionate and that is where my passion grew and that is where my passion for the subject began, and that is where I met my future wife, Ellen.

Ellen was seventeen and we fell in love. Ellen also came from a good family and was well read and versed in many subjects. Her father was Mr. David Thoreau who had lived in the south and helped organize an underground railroad to help slaves runaway. He is a Quaker and moved back up to Concord to join Mr. Emerson in his philosophical pursuits.

We shared a love for music. She played the piano, and we both fell in love with all the ideas that swirled in the esteemed company of Waldo Emerson's house.

Suddenly it all changed. Ellen was pregnant with our first child when Scarlet Fever swept through. Ellen died the same week that Waldo Emerson's first child died of the same affliction. We were all devastated. My world had been swept away. I took the journals of Mr. David Thoreau and vowed to go south and help slaves runaway to their freedom. I was so young then. I had just turned 21.

I dove into my studies and graduated Divinity School and vowed to devote my life to the abolition of slavery. I vowed never to remarry. Soon, I grew weary of the drawing room discussions of abolition and thought about what action I could take. I was being considered an eccentric and was ostracized by Emerson's social circle, and Ellen's parents partly blamed me for her death because she was so young.

One day I just packed a rucksack and I just started walking. I left Concord and I left the idea of a comfortable life behind. I took a little of my money, just enough to aid me in my travels. It was late spring. The war was still four years off. It took me a couple months to get down to Richmond. For a while, I stayed with people and relatives of people I met at Harvard. They were curious, and questioned me about this drastic undertaking, but understood after my great loss. I told them of my plans or a lack of plans, but wanted to help slaves escape. I took names and addresses from these people of wealth who might be of service to me at some later date. Most were very much against slavery, but didn't want to be involved at the level I might require which was understandable. Most were of a political nature, but they were all talk and no action. I also had contacts my father-in-law gave me, but these were more than thirty years old, but his contacts in Salem, North Carolina would still be of use because of the Quaker community.

Ben

I felt like a hunted animal with survival the only goal. I made a wild dash to the thicket and into the woods. I veered away from the battle and ran and ran until I was back behind our lines. I swam across the river and hid along the bank until darkness fell and I tried to formulate a plan. If they caught me, they would hang me as an example of what happens to deserters, or if I was lucky they would shoot me. I was somewhere in northern Virginia at a place called Manassas and would have to make the long trek back to the mountains. I would wait until darkness to travel the road west and then only travel at night. I had a few days' provisions in my knapsack, then I'd have to forage for food. Based on our march here from Raleigh, I figured it would take me a couple weeks to get home. I knew one thing. I was done with this war and I was done with people and if I could make it back to the mountains, that's where I would stay.

As darkness fell, the cries of the wounded carried across the orchards and fields. It sounded like a hundred dying beasts. It was indescribable, and I still hear those pitiful cries to this day. The cries for water and help echoed in the eerie silence of what deafening agony had happened here earlier.

The next morning I wasn't sure yet where I was. Somewhere behind our lines as there was a confusion of men and horses moving in the chaos of the first big battle. I stopped by the side of the road and there was a ragged little girl of maybe eight or nine sitting in a ditch with what appeared to be a fiddle case, of all things.

Ben

Hallo, you. What's a little girl doing sitting here all by herself?

Girl

My pappy and me live just up the road there. Yesterday we were visited by a cannon ball. It was a polite cannon ball cause it came in through the backdoor and through our kitchen.

Ben

Well, I'm sure sorry to hear that. Me, I got visited by a butt of a rifle up side of my head. This war ain't fer the likes of you and me. Where's yer Pappy?

Girl

Second cannonball weren't so polite. It killed my Pappy and house near burnt down.

Ben

You got any relations nearby that can help ye out?

Girl

Nah, sir. We just moved up here from a little place called Appomattox. You ever heard of it?

Ben

Can't say that I have? Is that a fiddle you got there?

Girl

Yes sir. It was my Pappy's. He didn't play though. He thought he would, but he was all the time startin things and then not finishing them. That's why we moved around a lot. The house was burning down, so I had to grab something on the way out. Too bad it was this fiddle. You want it?

Ben

Oh I couldn't take yer fiddle. It's all you got.

Girl

I don't want it. Can you play it?

Ben
Well, yes. By the way, I'm a fair to middlin fiddle player. Learned from my Pappy. I tell ya what. I got a dollar here. This sorry ass war has paid me a dollar to try and kill people I don't even know and as I see it, it's going to kill me first, so don't tell nobody but I'm heading back home.

Girl
Hit's a deal. I thankee kindly.

Ben
Mind if I look at it. . . My, my, that's nice work. Hey, here comes a detail of officers riding down the road. I'll flag em down. Maybe they can help you out.

Wilson
Whoa, there. You a wounded soldier?

Ben
Yes sir. Head wound, but I stopped you because I got this little girl here who lost her father and her home. I was wondering if you could help her out.

Wilson
Right. What your name, girl?

Girl
Lucy.

Wilson
Well. Lucy. You remind me of my little sister back home. . . We'll take care of her, soldier. Corporal, take her up to headquarters.

Jackson
You a fiddle player, son?

Ben
Yes sir.

Jackson
You wounded in the head?

Ben
Yes sir. Butt of a rifle got me.

Jackson
Come with me. I need a fiddle player for a dinner we're having
tonight. My other fiddle player got killed today. God rest his fiddling
soul. You know who I am, son?

Ben
No sir. I'm kind of new here.

Jackson
My name Jackson. General Thomas Jackson. I earned the name
"Stonewall" today. Thanks to my brave men and the everlasting Lord.
So boy, remember my name. What's my name, boy?

Ben
Andrew Jackson, sir.

Jackson
Not Andrew Jackson, you nitwit. That blow on the head has left
you daft.

Ben
Sorry, General, my daddy knew Andrew Jackson back in the day.
That must a been it. General, may I ask why you're holding your right
arm up in the air like that?

Jackson
It settles the blood and excites the humours when I ride into battle
under the banner of heaven. What's my name?

Ben
General Thomas Jackson, or Stonewall.

Jackson
Correct. Now don't forget. Now come with us.

Wilson
You're lucky you're a fiddle player. General Jackson has a soft spot
for fiddle players, and General Jackson doesn't have any soft spots. He
was just as likely to have you shot as a deserter since you are wandering
behind our lines. Where's your regiment?

Ben
I don't know, sir. I got separated in the smoke and confusion and
then I got hit in the head, and when I came to, there was a dead soldier
on top of me.

Wilson
Well, you're lucky you don't play the banjo. General Jackson hates
the banjo. Hey, you have a certain drawl in your speech where you
from?

Ben
I was raised in the west part of North Carolina, up in the mountains.

Wilson

Well, doggone. I was born in the self same mountains, up in
Madison County. How bout them apples?

Ben

It's a small world ain't it.

Wilson

Well, come with me. You can bunk with me for a night or two. I left
those mountains quite a few years ago. I bet you got some tales.

Ben

Well, it will be nice to have someone to talk to. A lot of people I met
got killed in the battle.

Wilson

Well, well, a mountain boy. You come on with me.

CHAPTER 27

You're Not in Kansas Anymore

Andrew

By late summer, I landed in Harper's Ferry, a little town at the confluence of the Shenandoah and Potomac rivers. I began to camp or stay in boarding houses, meeting people of all social classes, and talking to them in taverns or churches, or the boarding houses, or wherever. By then, I had a shock of long hair and a beard, and was mostly taken for a well-spoken vagabond. I also talked to freedmen and women and slaves when I got a chance to try to understand them as people. I was in uncharted territory in every aspect of my character, and like my journey, was guided as much by intuition and purpose, as opposed to any real plan or destination.

After about a year of traveling, I found myself wishing to stay here for a while. A small, thriving town, I decided to set up a little church and rest for a spell as winter was coming on. I found a small cabin I rented from a kindly widow, and a meeting room in the basement of a school. I found a few people who were not put off by my yankee ways. I did not reveal my education or background as I wanted to live among the people I might could help. After a month or so, I had a small congregation of fifteen displaced Quakers. The liberal nature of my sermons made me most suspicious, and my abolitionist views were not well accepted outside my small group. But I was not ardent about it in my day to day operations, and I found people here that were accepting of other people as long as it didn't become a subject of passionate debate. My purpose was to listen and to learn.

One evening a disheveled bearded fellow walked into the small gathering and with piercing blue eyes he spoke like a man possessed.

John Brown
I just walked from Kansas.

Andrew
Well, sir, welcome. That's a far piece.

John Brown
Kansas, I tell ya.

Andrew
Well, sir, this isn't Kansas anymore.

John
No, this is Eden's Gate, and I'm here to start an uprising among the slaves. To rid the world of this evil. Men claiming to be christians, yet owning other humans. It is an abomination, and I have been called by God to lead the revolt.

Andrew
Well, sir, you will find that the friends here will agree with you on the evils of slavery, but we are a peaceful congregation that condemns violence.

John
God has spoken to me. He said leave Kansas.

Andrew
Maybe God doesn't like Kansas.

John
He spoke to me and said come here to the heart of slavery. There is an arsenal of weapons there. Gather up slaves, and arm them, and overthrow this corrupt system. All of you with me raise your right arm.

Andrew
Well, sir you seem to be the only one holding your arm up like that.

John
Fool! I am not raising my hand. I hold my arm like this because it settles the blood and aligns the constitution. You don't know where I can find a good used horse do you?

Andrew
Well, you can try the livery stable.

John
Thank you. I will be on my way now. Remember my name--John Brown.

Andrew
We'll try, But that is an awful common name. Anyway, good luck in your endeavors.

****

Ben
So I became the personal fiddle player of Thomas Stonewall Jackson in the Army of Northern Virginia all the while planning my desertion and escape. Jackson was crazy as hell which made him a brilliant general, I suppose. But in the spring of 1862 he marched us into the Shenadoah

Valley which only got me closer to home. I was only a hundred miles or so down the Blue Ridge to my home in North Carolina. I would bide my time and then escape into the mountains. Until then, we marched and we marched and we marched some more, engaging the Union Army a few times. The poor men were exhausted, but Jackson drove them like horses. I'm just glad I was just carrying a fiddle, and Jackson's bible, which was considerable heavier than my fiddle. I don't know why he took to me. He once said I reminded him of Jesus. Also, "Onward Christian Soldiers" on the fiddle got him revved up for battle.

Jackson
Now, gentlemen, let us bow our heads and pray, "Dear God, the enemy of freedom and woeful sinners is at our door and we must smite them. . .

Sergeant
General Jackson, sir. We captured five men deserting the battlefield. What should we do with them?

Jackson
Hang them.

Sergeant
Yes sir.

Jackson
Dear Lord, give us courage in this hour, and mercy when it is deserved, but mostly let us smite the enemy a terrible blow.

Captain
General Jackson, sir. We just captured ten Union soldiers from the picket line. What should we do with them?

Jackson
Shoot them.

Jackson
Dear God, Help us through these trials and show love if we've got nothing better to do. And yes, give us your terrible swift sword to smite the enemy, and Lord let my horses run free in fields of. . . and my wife at home. . and oh well, I lost my train of thought. Amen.

Ben
Amen.

Jackson
Now let the men sleep tonight, but we march first thing tomorrow to Port Royal to smite the enemy.

Ben
That was it for me. They was going back north in the wrong direction. So tonight I would steal away into the mountains. Jackson would be too excited about the grueling march and battle to look for me. I would be gone and smite-proof.

Wilson
That little girl you gave us. We found her a nice widow lady to stay with up near Winchester. I took her myself when we were scouting the river crossings. I'm an engineer by training. We sure do have to cross a lot of rivers, so we have to construct a lot of bridges. The way Jackson keeps us moving. I'll be glad when I'm done with General Stonewall Jackson.

Ben
That girl gave me that fiddle. Said it belonged to her dead pappy.

Wilson

She saved your life then, and maybe you saved hers by stopping us on the road. I tell you there's something special about that girl. I have a mind to go back and adopt her myself, cept ain't nobody knows how long this war will last. If I was a betting man, I'd say we're in for a long haul.

CHAPTER 28

Ariella Isabella

Andrew
I stayed in Harper's Ferry for a year but became restless and moved south to Salem, North Carolina, and looked up some of the former contacts of my father in law, David Thoreau. They befriended me and gave me a place to stay. I stayed with Abigail and Joshua Stanley. The underground railroad was already in operation and the Stanley's were a station. I stayed with them for four months and made several contacts. Ultimately, they convinced me to move west into the mountains near Asheville where I could set up a station. They informed me there was a network of abolitionists in western North Carolina and eastern Tennessee.

Abigail
Mr. Milton, did you happen to know a Mr. David Thoreau while living in Concord?

Andrew
Why. what a funny coincidence, Mrs. Stanley, I not only knew him but I married his daughter. Sadly, she died of Scarlet Fever a year ago. That is why I have come to devote my life to the abolition of slavery, and the teachings of Mr. Thoreau.

Joshua

We are so sorry to hear about your wife. You must know that Mr.
Thoreau was a leading figure in the Quaker community here in Salem,
and helped organize our underground railroad for runaway slaves.

Andrew

Yes, I know. I've come to help continue his work.

Joshua

That is excellent to hear, Mr. Milton. We will help set you up in the
mountains a couple days' ride west of here. You'll become a station for
runaways.

Andrew

Yes, please tell me all you know. I spent many evenings listening to
Mr. Thoreau and Waldo Emerson discuss nature and philosophy.

Abigail

Here she is! Andrew, this is Ariella Isabella. She came to us last year
from Texas. She is an orphan. She is Mexican. One of our friends took
pity on her and brought her here to Salem. We're looking for someone
to adopt her.

Andrew

When I get settled in the mountains, I would be interested. I'm
alone and to tell you the truth, she reminds me so much of my deceased
wife. Darker complected, of course, but still there is something about
her. Something in her eyes. What is your name again, child?

Ariella

My name is Ariella Isabella.

Abigail
Well, I don't know. We'll have to see. She hasn't been with us long. She repeats her name a lot, but says little else. Poor child has been traumatized, and she doesn't speak much English. She was found by the river. We have no papers. We have no idea who she really is.

Ariella
My name is Ariella Isabella.

The strange man with the red hair and pale skin asks me my name. I didn't blink. I didn't think. I was five years old. I said Ariella Isabella. That was not my name. I was found by the river and brought to the orphanage after they found me sitting by the Rio Grande river. I was waiting for my father to come and get me. He never came. He drowned in the river, they said, although they didn't know for sure. The night before he had told me a story that came in the form of a song while I was going to sleep by the campfire. He said in a dream a beautiful senorita had come to him and told him her name. "Ariella Isabella," she said, as I was drifting off into my own dream. A dream within a dream.

I stared at the strange man who was going to adopt me. Whatever that means. I wasn't afraid. He had kindness in his eyes, and that is why I told him I was Ariella Isabella.

Stanley
Well, it's late. You should get some sleep before your journey tomorrow. We'll talk more in the morning. Yes, what is it dear?

Ariella
My name is Ariella Isabella. I'll go with the man.

Abigail
My goodness. Well, go to bed, dear. We'll talk about it in the morning.

Sally's Diary (June 1862)

Well, glory be the day. I woke up this morning and guess who I saw coming down the path? It was our son, Ben. Our only son come home from the war. It's funny, I was just finishing my fourteenth novel where a soldier deserts his Army in the war with Napoleon and comes home. Again, the way real life intrudes on my story. Sometimes I don't know who is doing the writing here.

He was tired, but all in one piece. Davy and I assured him we'd hide him if anyone came looking, and no one was going to come looking up in these mountains. I know no one here much cared about the war. It seemed impossibly faraway. Davy and I were 70 years old now and no spring chickens, even our chickens weren't spring chickens. Our mule was so old, sometimes Davy had to carry him. I'm kidding you about that. That's an old Jack Tale that Davy likes to tell. Davy and Ben will start to build a little cabin down in the cove for a hiding place.

Andrew

The next morning, Joshua and Abigail and I took care of the arrangements for where I was going, and arrangements for Ariella Isabella who seemed to be relieved to be coming with me. I was not sure why. I wasn't sure of anything at that point, and adopting a Mexican child, I didn't know, it just seemed to deepen the mystery and confusion of what I was doing. On my way west, We stopped at a small plantation near Marion that also served as a stage coach inn and a boarding house, so I took a room there. I put a small pallet on the floor for Ariella to sit on. She didn't speak, but just looked knowingly out of her big dark eyes that reminded me so much of my dead wife.

The Carson's had a small plantation in the Catawba River valley about ten miles east of Old Fort. They were, by far, the largest slave holding family in the area. Joshua and Abigail told me it would be a good place to make some contacts and that is how I met Joseph. The

Carson's had about 60 slaves and grew tobacco and corn. They made a lot of whiskey and it was the social center of the area. One of the sons ran the plantation now and they took in boarders as well. The family were devout Methodists and held camp meetings on the grounds.

During the few days that I stayed there, I was free to wander the grounds. One afternoon, I heard a banjo down near the large barn by the creek. A light-skinned negro was playing the banjo. Ariella seemed enthralled by it and she took my hand and led me to the music.

Andrew
That's a mighty fine banjo playing, sir.

Joseph
Thank ye, kindly. You here for the camp meeting I reckon, since I ain't never seen you before?

Andrew
Yes, My name is Andrew Milton. I'm from up north. Just moved down and was staying with some Quaker friends in Salem. This is my brand new daughter, Ariella Isabella.

Joseph
You don't say. You them folks that shake and speak in tongues when possessed by the spirit of the Lord.

Andrew
Well, actually, no. I think the name doesn't do us justice. We are more rational and consider peace the most important thing, and we are very much against slavery.

Joseph
You don't say. I wouldn't overshare that information round here. Get ya in trouble. I was born in it, but momma, Kadella, they brought her over on a ship. My name Joseph, by the way.

Andrew
Nice to meet you, Joseph. I'm going to be moving up into the
mountains above Old Fort here. Got a cabin. I'll be talking to you
again.

****

Kadella
Lord, Lord. Come in, outa this rain. Joseph what you doing walking these people through the rain?

Joseph
It's okay, momma. This here Andrew and his brand new daughter,
Ariella Isabella.

Kadella
Is it now? Brand new? What, she just drop out of the sky or somethin?

Andrew
No, mam. She's orphaned and I adopted her when I was in Salem.
I'm moving up in the mountains, and well, it's a long story, but she's
my child now.

Kadella
Everything a long story, eventually. What you think about that
child?

Ariella
My name is Ariella Isabella?

Kadella
You a special child. I can tell, and look at those beautiful brown
eyes. You a preacher, Andrew?

Andrew
Kind of?

Kadella
You a kinda of preacher? And you got a daughter that dropped
outta the sky. Must be a long story.

Joseph
Andrew here to help people. Wants to help us slaves.

Kadella
For real, or kinda of help. Ain't much help until this dreadful war
over and seems from what I hear it's just gettin started.

Joseph
We thought it okay if Ariella sleep in your cabin tonight with you.

Kadella
If it's okay with Ariella, it okay with me.

Ariella
My name is Ariella Isabella.

CHAPTER 29

The Night I Ran Away From Slavery and Bones Tells a Story

Joseph

The night I ran away from slavery the quarter moon sat crooked in the east like a cradle. Just enough crooked light to make my way west along the river. Another slave, named Bones, who lives at the Greenlee place just west of the Carson House came with me. We knew each other from the camp meetings, and I sure was glad for the company. I followed the river. I knew the way. The river knew the way. It sang its way east toward the crooked moon, but I was going upstream, moving against time and the future. We would have three nights to travel before they knew we was gone.

We was scared and we moved fast, occasionally stumbling on a root that just propelled us forward into the past. The late summer midnight was full of life and sound. The insects sang in the key of the river, and I moved like the panther. Quietly and quickly over the open fields toward the settlement of Old Fort where we would sleep deep in the woods during the heat of the day. Then the next night along Mill Creek into the mountains.

We was scared. If they caught us, they would beat us, ship us off to work in their gold mine or worse. Tomorrow night the crooked moon would put on another layer of light that would barely penetrate the rising mountain forest along Mill Creek up into the mountains. Up into the unknown.

Bones

It awful dark. You shore you know where you going? If I bump into one more tree, I'm just gonna let it knock me over and I'll go to sleep under it. Speakin of sleep, shouldn't we be doing some of that?

Joseph

We gotta make it to the waterfall tonight. We close. Hear it?

Bones

Twixt, the wind and the crickets, and critters and my own breathing, I don't know what I'm hearing. Did you ever hear the story bout Brother Rabbit escaping from the Devil?

Joseph

Well, if you stop talking you can hear a little better. Listen, I can hear it. It up this way. We have to climb up around these rocks.

Bones

Well, you know, Brother Rabbit, he smarter than all the other critters, but now the Devil he smarter too. One day, he caught Brother Rabbit in his devil's rabbit trap. Devil liked nothin better than boiled rabbit.

Joseph

Bones, shush, you can tell me the story when we reach the waterfall. Devil be the least of our worries if we lose time, or get lost.

Bones

I'm scared, and when I scared I need to talk, just like Brother Rabbit
did. When the devil come up on Brother Rabbit in that trap, Brother
Rabbit start talking, and telling the devil that if he didn't eat him, he'd
give him his soul and it could start a whole new business for him.
Collecting people's souls could give him access to all the rabbits he'd
ever want fer forever, or even longer maybe. Now all the time, Brother
Rabbit twisting his foot around to try to squeeze out of the jaws of
that trap.

Joseph

It darker than the inside of a panther in these woods. I hear the
water fall. Come on, it's this way.

Bones

The devil pondered that notion. "People's souls, hmm? That could
be a lucrative trade. Yes. But a rabbit's soul? I'll ponder it, but I don't
ponder too well on an empty stomach, so after I boil you and eat you.
I'll think about it, but thank ye Brother Rabbit fer the suggestion."

Joseph

Good, look! We're here! We'll sleep over here under that tree.
Speaking of food, I gotta little deer jerky left in my pack. We can get
some sleep and travel by day tomorrow. We should be in a day's walk to
Andrew's. Go on now, finish the story. What happened?

Bones

Well, during that time, Brother Rabbit, had clean worked his foot
plumb off, and when the devil turned around to get his pot ready.
Brother Rabbit hopped off and got a way from the very Devil himself.
And that's why a rabbit's foot is good luck. I got one right here I carry
with me.

Joseph

Ha! That's a right good story, and now I'm getting drowsy so we
ought to get some sleep.

Bones

Yep, and the Lord was so impressed with Brother Rabbit that he
allowed Brother Rabbit's foot to grow right back like nothin never
even happened. Yep, gettin right sleepy myself. Good night, Brother
Joseph.

****

Joseph

When we got to the cabin, we thought it was Andrew's. It
was just before dawn on the fourth day of our escape. We were
fugitives now, and word would be spreading. The sky was just
beginning to lean into the coming light as the world tilted and
turned. We lay on our stomachs at the edge of the pasture and
waited. We was close enough, if I saw Andrew and his shock of
red hair, I would recognize him. It had been just a few weeks
since I'd met him at the Carson House, and he told me of the
underground network north.

Someone was up, as smoke curled out of the chimney and
into the faint light of dawn. We waited. Someone opened the
cabin door and called to the livestock. It was the young girl
with dark hair and eyes that had been with Andrew at the
plantation. It meant the coast was clear. A few minutes later, I
saw him. His red hair and beard glinting in the sunrise, and I
knew I had arrived. He would hide us.

CHAPTER 30

Fourteen Years Gone By and She'll Be Coming Round the Mountain When She Comes

Andrew's Journal--July 5, 1877

Ariella has turned into a fine, young woman. She has just turned 17. We didn't know her birth date, so I picked March 17, the anniversary of my marriage to Ellen. In young womanhood, Ariella bears an uncanny likeness to Ellen, in her beauty and demeanor. She loves nature and she sings beautifully, although she is a bit delinquent in her studies. Joseph and I both have tried to teach her, but she won't sit still for long.

We have lived in our mountain cabin now for twelve years. I have just passed my 40th year. Along with Joseph, I helped twenty slaves run away to the north. It is work I'm very proud of. Now I travel and minister around the area to revivals and churches, but I'm happiest here at home.

Joseph escaped not long after I met him. He was my first slave to stop at my station. We hid him deep in the cove in an abandoned cabin we fixed up. We decided to let him stay as he contracted a fever and

Ariella was fond of him, and honestly, I was too, and we needed the help, having just moved into our cabin. In the confusion of the war, we didn't think anyone would come looking for him.

We were isolated on a little mountain and valley miles from the turnpike that wound up the mountain to Asheville. There was a small community of cabins separated by miles. Joseph lived deep in the cove hidden by rhododendron along Rock Creek. Our cabin was a little further up the ridge along a trail that we could take to the turnpike. Ben, who had deserted from the confederate army in 1862, lived up on top of the mountain. His mother and father had lived there for a long time and I knew them briefly before they passed away. Then there's Elizabeth, a widow, who lives between us and Ben. We have small gatherings here from time to time. Mostly to visit, and to share the food we have, and play music. Joseph plays banjo and the strange little thumb piano Kadella had given him before he ran away. Ariella sings the Irish and Scottish songs everyone here seems to know. Ben is a wonderful fiddle player like his father, but the war has left him traumatized and he doesn't always come around. He is essentially a hermit. All of these folks are blessings to know and have as company. Joseph is a few years older than me and Ben is too. Elizabeth is younger. Perhaps in her early 30's.

Lately, the chats have turned to the coming of the road. Not a road exactly, but a train track up the mountain to Asheville. Everyone is against it here, except Ariella. They ran away from this world for good reason and now they fear the world is coming to them. I have picked up magazines and newspapers on my ministering trips and know it is inevitable. It would have been built years before except for two things: the Civil War had depleted--labor and money. Recently, the legislature has found a solution--prison labor. There are plenty of prisoners and you don't have to pay them. Of course, it concerns me for its inhumanity. It is just slavery by another name, but I am resigned to it, so called progress is inevitable. I have seen the initial surveys and the planned route and it winds up the mountain over passes and through tunnels miles away from us. The prisoners will be housed in stockades built near Old Fort and further up as the road makes progress.

****

The Road

I am the road that has not been built. I am waiting. I've been charted and marked off. I am an idea lying beneath the surface of trees and rock that are a million years old. Soon poor men will come with picks and shovels and axes, and some will use flat stones for they are just animals of the earth--beasts and laborers. I am the track that has not been laid. The trees will be cleared. Tunnels will have to be built, and the mountain will be cut and cry out the million years and give way to the next million years. I lie in wait because progress never sleeps. Destruction precedes construction, and I lie like a sleeping, giant serpent that will coil up this mountain and choke it, and subdue into another kind of life.

Wilson's first letter (Oct. 1876)

My dearest Louisa,

I know you did not want me to take this job, and leave you and the children for what may well be a long period of time. The engineering challenge of building a railroad up this mountain is daunting and will test me in various ways. I hope you understand, my dear, that duty has called me away.

We arrived here at Henry Station on the morning of October 12. It is a flat piece of land by Mill Creek just west of the settlement of Old Fort. It is rather desolate as they are clearing more land and beginning to construct the barracks that will house the convicts. It is a daunting task to build a railroad up a mountain. I am not sure it can be done, but I have been tasked to do it by the governor no less. Now we must gather mules, horses, tools; such as, axes and shovels, and provide provisions for the coming convicts—all of which will provide a huge challenge. We have laid out the route, but the thought of building trestles and tunnels and navigating the grade in these mountains will prove difficult.

I am sorry darling that I did not allow you to come with me when you asked, but the thought of having you here in such a primitive place and with 300 convicts due in a week or two, it was unfathomable. I know you worry we will grow apart and the project may take a year or more. I promise to have you come for extended visits when the place and project gets up and going. Maybe I can rent a small house in Old Fort. Building the railroad up this mountain and being assigned by our governor was too big a challenge and duty for me to turn down. I do hope you understand. Kiss the children for me.

Yours always,

Jim

Ariella
Andrew, how long will it take them to build it, before the first train steams up the mountain?

Andrew
It will take them years I suspect to complete it. Two years or so.

Ariella
That's a long time.

Andrew
Yes. It's a monumental task. Perhaps you will be away at school by then.

Ariella
I'm not going away to school. My school is here. The mountains and trees and the music. You and Joseph are my teachers. I can read and write and figure. I'm smart. Will they teach me about Mr. Emerson?

Andrew
All that is true, my dear. But soon you'll have no prospects here. It would be good for you to experience what the world has to offer. I

would not be here with you now had I not traveled, and searched for my calling.

Ariella
Well, what if my calling is right here?

Andrew
Well, we will see in due time. Maybe the train will carry you off. Perhaps you will stay close. Asheville maybe, or Raleigh, or maybe here. You are young. You don't want to be stuck here with all us old people. The world is changing fast.

Ariella
They are using convicts to build the train?

Andrew
Yes.

Ariella
What will the convicts be like? And how many will they need?

Andrew
I don't know. Hundreds maybe. They will be men almost exclusively. And they will be black men mostly.

Ariella
Why?

Andrew
Why? Well, those are the men who are in prison. And they are in prison mostly because they are black. It is not a fair system, but it is the way that it is.

Ariella

And that is the world you want to send me into?

Andrew

Well, it is not all bad. And we must do what good we can as well as
find happiness. What would Emerson say?

Ariella

I don't know. He reads too slow for me. What will the convicts be
like? Will we see them?

CHAPTER 31

The Convicts

Jimmy

The first thing I remember is a song. The first place-- a rickety porch. The first sound-- a guitar strummed. The first smell--my mother's sweet breath. Then my mother's voice singing, sweet and low. "Swing low, sweet chariot." I did not understand the words, but I understood the sound. The language of sound into song into melody. It floats on the air like smoke, or mountain mist rising. I was born into the world then, a different world.

My mother was a teacher and we lived where everyone was a share-cropper. Slavery by a different name. But I remember sitting on that porch with my uncles, that's what I called them. I never knew who my father was. My mother had been a slave, but when the war ended, she ended up with one of her uncles near Nashville. She learned that Fisk University was training freed blacks as teachers to go out into the countryside and set up schools. She also sang with their choir.

She ended up here with a different uncle, and set up a school on what was a former plantation near Raleigh. I was born before the war in 1857. We lived in a old slave cabin outside Smithville, tobacco country, Klan country. They burned down my mother's first one room school because they didn't want negroes to learn to read and write.

Beulah

I remember everything. I even remember being born. I even remember hearing my mother singing while I rode in her belly as she picked cotton in the field. I don't think it was the muffled sound of her voice, but the melody rising and falling. People tell me I'm crazy. People don't remember when they're born or before, but that's all right, I know what I remember. It's a gift. Music gave me the gift, and I sing all the time. I am crazy and I drive other people crazy. I was working in a house in Raleigh. A rich man, and a rich woman, who seemed to remember nothing, or feel nothing, or hear any music at all. Nothing but the sound of money. The more they did: drinking, dancing, having big parties, the less they seemed to feel.

The man had his eye on me and desired me because I sang and I remembered everything. The wife became jealous, and the one thing they did feel was jealousy, hatred, contempt for people who loved their songs because they could not love, not even with all the money in the world.

Jimmy

My mother taught me to sing and read, in that order. She also taught me how to play the white man. "Keep your eyes down. Don't look them in the eye. Say, yes sir, no sir. Think how much you despise them, but don't show it. Listen carefully. There are many whites who are good at heart and know this way is wrong and will be kind to you. Listen and find them. You will know the ones to hate and hate them with all your heart, and be patient and wait. Get in their good favor and then you can use that to your advantage. We must be like the rabbit in the stories. We have no power so we must use our wiles, and play their game to use against them." My mother, god bless her, I did all those things and I still went to jail for nothing and here I am on this chain gang building a railroad up a mountain.

Jimmy
That you, Bones? I hope that you rubbin up against me?

Bones
It me. We squeezed in this here boxcar with 30 men bouncing down
the tracks.

Jimmy
Well, just stay here. I'm up against the wall with my gui-tar trying to
keep it from gettin smashed.

Bones
The only good thing about being squeezed in here is we been
traveling fer a couple hours now, and I'm dead tired, but they so many
people in here you can't lay down, but everybody holding everybody
else up. And it dark in here. Darker than the inside of a cow.

Jimmy
Probably don't want to see. I just wish we'd get to wherever we're
going.

Bones
Did ye see that boxcar they was loading the women convicts in. I
wish I was in that boxcar.

Jimmy
What we doing building a railroad straight up a mountain? We just
slaves is all.

Bones
How many convicts on this train?

Jimmy
I counted ten boxcars?

Bones
Well, if there's 30 men to a boxcar and they ten boxcars. Let me
figure here. That's ten plus thirty plus another thirty. That's a. . .? It's a
big flock a convicts.

Jimmy
Three hundred, Bones. That would be three hundred.

Bones
Right. I was just arriving at that sum. Starlight, wake up, quit
snoring in my ear.

Starlight
Oh Bones, I was dreaming I was up in my tree. Drinking the stars.
****

Beulah
Bertie, that you? It so dark and dank in this God damned boxcar.
What are we, cows? They cram us in a God damned boxcar and be
shipping us to God knows where, to do God knows what?

Bertie
I don't feel so good, Beulah. I feel like I'm going to be sick.

Beulah
Don't you dare puke in this boxcar. Ain't no where fer it to go. Why
they need us to build a railroad up a mountain?

Bertie

They need us to cook and clean fer all these men, I reckon. I think I
gotta lay down, Beulah.

Beulah

Don't you sink down, girl. Ain't no room. You be trampled down
there. Here just lean up against me. Just don't puke. Close your eyes.
We'll be there soon. Then we can get out of this God damned boxcar.

****

Jimmy

Hey, Starlight. Look at all these trees. You get yer pick if they ever let
ya out of the stockade.

Starlight

I'm just glad we're out of that boxcar. Morning sure is bright. I
can't see nuthin'.

Bones

Sure is a lot a convicts in one place. Why all these crackers lined up
staring at us? Ain't they never seen a convict before.

Jimmy

Not this many in one place. Excuse us, folks. We ain't had time to
freshen up from our train ride cause we were crammed in a God
damned boxcar. And it ain't that we're convicts. It because we're black
men. They never seen this many black men.

Starlight

Or any black people. Look at these trees.

****

Beulah

In a boxcar, in a God damned boxcar like we were just animals, and to many of them that's what we are. Animals work for white people for free. That's all they wanted. Someone to do their dirty work for free. Make more money that way.

They worked us hard the first week--cooking, cleaning. Every few days, in the morning they'd march us down to the creek and we'd have to bathe in that cold water. The guards would make us get naked so they could leer at us, and make fun of us.

Jimmy

Cuse me. Where you want me to set these dishes?

Beulah

Just set'em there on the table. We gettin ready to take them down to the creek.

Jimmy

I heard ya singin when I came in. It sounded real nice.

Beulah

It wasn't me. Nope. You must of misheard.

****

Jimmy

Swing the ax. Whack! The morning passes as the sun rises high, and clear above the ridges about mid-day. Th-whack. The metal ax on tree trunk makes a note that hums and resonates through the air. I couldn't get her out of my head, or her song. I tried to make up a song to go with her tune. Th-whack! To the rhythm of the ax. I might have a little time to mess with it on my guitar when we finish for the day. . . "Hey, Bones. How long we been here now?"

Bones

Let's see? Let me figure. . . Ten boxcars?

Jimmy

Never mind. I think we been here bout a month. I've
counted bout 30 days.

Bones

Bout the same as convicts in a boxcar. Long enough to be
sick of all this digging.

Starlight

Least you got a shovel. I'm having to use this ol flat rock.

Bones

Starlight, let me tell ya, you ain't much with a shovel, anyway. You just keep swinging that flat rock and don't work too
hard. You'll be alright. And Jimmy, my friend, I been a convict
a spell longer than you, and counting the days is something I
stopped doing a long time ago. It's just the day you in and
that's bout it. No matter how bad the day is, they another one
just round the corner, so no need to rush it.

Jimmy

They say they going to let us play music on Saturday nights
soon. Let us blow off some steam. I got my guitar ready and
you got your banjo and Starlight his drum. Maybe get that gal
to sing.

Bones

That kitchen gal you sweet on?

Jimmy

I ain't sweet on her, yet. But she pretty and she can sing,
though she ain't too friendly right now.

****

Beulah

Survival. That's all it is I guess. Caged animals, but you
learn to survive. It ain't living exactly, but you adapt as you try
to figure things out. Some people don't make it. Some people
die, but that ain't you. That's somebody else. I met Bertie. She
a young black girl like me. They thirty of us convict women
here and about 300 men. We got each other's back. We bunk
`up and try to stay together because there's some older, meaner
convict women in here who is jealous of us, I guess. We get
extra attention from the guards, but we don't want it. You
gotta team up here with somebody if you're gonna survive.

Bertie

They sayin they gonna be a party on Saturday with music
and such. Did you hear that? You gonna sing?

Beulah

I ain't heard nothin like that. Them taters Im peelin don't
talk much. I ain't singin fer nobody but me.

Bertie

Land's sake. Why you like that? You sing like an angel. If I
could sing like you, I'd be singing all the time. I'd be like that
tree climbing fool, Starlight. He's all the time singing. He a
sweet boy.

Beulah

That boy get you killed some day. Acting crazy. I just don't
fancy singin fer people. That's all.

****

Bones

"Once upon a time, there was Brother Rabbit," said Brother Rabbit. That's you, Jimmy, young, handsome, smart, you knows how to play the white man. Wilson already knows your name, knows you can read and write. And Brother Rabbit gathered all the critters together. Brother Bear, that's me, big, dumb, but not as dumb as people think, and good hearted, ready for anything, best friend to Brother Rabbit.

Jimmy

You ain't dumb. You just ain't educated. There's a difference. For as I can tell, you the smartest one here. Playing dumb is a smart strategy, and you the storyteller. Every group needs a storyteller.

Bones

And then there was brother Crow. Everybody know the crow is the smartest of birds, except this one wasn't. This one was crazy, but crazy in a beautiful way. This crow smart in one world, but not the world he was in.

Jimmy

You talkin bout Starlight. He is crazy, but he can sure play any musical instrument you put in his hands. I even saw him play a table the other day. He play it so good it made the chair dance.

Starlight

That true. I made that chair dance on one leg. And Bones, could I be Brother Cardinal instead, cause then I get to dress all wild red and colorful?

Bones

Hey, who's telling the story here? I lost my train of thought. Get it? Train of thought. Anywho, Brother Rabbit gathered the other critters together, Brother Terrapin, Brother Fox, and Brother Possum, and told them they were going to start a band cause every place needed music. Well, Brother Bear said, "How we gonna do that, Brother Rabbit? We don't know what music is.." Well, that why we gonna make it, Brother Bear. We gonna bring it into the world. See, I stretched the string from this trap I found, and I tied it to this piece of wood and plucked it. I call this, banjo.

And Bear said, "And that is good." Rabbit says to Brother Bear, and you see these bones from the poor animal that was caught in the trap. Here, you snap these bones together, and they make a rhythm that can make a chair dance. And Bear said that was good.

And brother crow, here is a tiny instrument put together out of shiny metal pieces that came from handcuffs and prison bars, and you pluck it with your claws, and it makes a sound higher and sweeter than the banjo. We call it, kalimba. But above all, Crow, please don't sing because your voice sound like a rusty gate. And Bear said that was good.

And they formed a band and got tolerable good after a while, and that is how Brother Rabbit brought music into the world, and that's how we're forming a band. We got me, and you, and Starlight, and there's some other fellers wanting to play, and maybe we can get one of the gals to sing with us. Didn't you say you heard one of em singing real nice in the kitchen? Hit ain't gonna be that much fun watching a bunch of men convicts cutting a rug out there on Saturday.

CHAPTER 32

Ariella Meets Wilson and Laying the Track

Wilson

Dear Louisa,

Three hundred convicts in the first load. We built three stockades to house them. We've begun clearing the trees starting at Henry Station up Mill Creek--100 shovels, picks, and axes provided by the state, 57 mules and 40 horses. We bartered the locals for the rest. We hired forty men to help with the more skilled work: carpenters, masons, surveyors, men to set the charges. Most of the convicts will be negroes.

Yes, War hardens a man. I've seen plenty of men hanged. Black and white--deserters, runaways, petty criminals, and men who were at the wrong place at the wrong time. After the first few, I didn't avert my eyes. The signal, the release, the snap of the neck, I began to surmise the character of a man for how he died.

Men will die building this road. It is dangerous work. We won't hang anybody. We'll have to shoot a few, and there will be accidents, but I have a job to do. These are the men the state sent me. Expendable men. No more important than the mules. Less so probably.

How are the children? Tell them I love them and will see them soon.

Love always,

Jim

Ariella

My name is a song. I sing it every day. I hear it sung, "Ariella Isabella." I am seventeen now. I went down to Henry Station to see them start the road—the railroad up the mountain. Andrew and Joseph are against it. I don't know. Yesterday I heard the whippoorwill sing, "Ariella Isabellla." It was then I realized the world is calling me. You were born faraway from other people, from other places. The world is calling and I must answer.

It was a long walk there. It took me a couple hours, and I'd have to start back soon if I was to get back by nightfall, but I could follow the moon if need be. I saw a man there. A stern looking man who was directing this and directing that. I walked up to him. He didn't see me at first for he was talking to several other men about mules and axes, and gesturing and looking out at the path the road would make up the mountain. When he saw me, a young olive skinned girl, I think he mistook me for one of the convicts. He stopped and looked down at me with some irritation at the human interruption. I looked him in the eye and said, "My name is Ariella Isabella. I live a day's walk up on the mountain with my father. I think you could use me as a secretary or something. I'm looking for a job, and I'm awfully interested in trains and travel, and I know these mountains bout as well as anybody. My daddy is Preacher Andrew." The three men around him grinned at my nerve and the oddity of the situation. They looked toward the man who they thought would act angrily, but the man just stared back at me, held my gaze as if he saw something. He dismissed the three men, and they walked slowly off the porch, looking back, surprised by the boss's reaction.

Wilson

I know the girl. I mean, I don't know the girl, but I know her from somewhere in my past. She reminded me so much of the little girl I almost adopted. I was about her age thirty years ago. The way she just walked up and starting talking, and I saw in her eyes someone I knew. It was like seeing a ghost. I grew up in these mountains so long ago. I read, and schooled, and worked, and fought a war to get the mountains out of me. I succeeded all too well. But now I don't have time to dwell on the past. I'm long done with that. I did the math and mathed it out of me. Drew the map and I walked as far as I could from that meager, limited life. Took the nitroglycerin and blew those memories away like I'm going to blow this mountain down to build this road. I've got no time to dwell on what I erased even when the past walks up to you, and asks you for a job. But like this road I'm building, there will be tunnels, and like all these washed out memories, there are always tunnels with just a little bit of light that you can't block out. So she wants to work for me, but now where did she go? Maybe she is a ghost.

Ariella

I walked home along the wide destruction of the road in its beginnings. Men were working. Mostly black men. I had never seen so many black men. I had seen a few and helped Andrew help some of them escape slavery when I was a little girl, but other than Joseph, I didn't see many black men in these hills. I walked along up the grade and curves of the road until I was ready to turn onto the narrow natural path that ran along a stream for several miles. Some of the men noticed me and stared blankly, but most just kept working. Some were laying the first bit of heavy steel track onto the gravel bed. They were singing. Chanting in rhythm as they moved together to move the heavy steel. I stopped just outside the trail and listened to the rough, beautiful sound. The call and response. I'll remember to tell Andrew. He will be interested cause he collects all kinds of songs and might be familiar with some of them.

Jimmy

I noticed the girl right away. There was something about her. I had seen some of the mountain girls and women on the day I arrived, crammed into the boxcar with the other convicts. Thirty to a car. I managed to squeeze in against the wall of the car, so I could protect my old guitar. When the train finally stopped, we poured out of that car and breathed in the fresh mountain air. I filled my lungs and I exhaled, closed my eyes, and never imagined something as simple as breathing would feel so good. When I opened my eyes to look around, there was a crowd of local and mountain people standing near the train cars gawking at us. I gawked back. We were a spectacle to them. They had never seen so many black men before, and convicts to boot. We were the circus arriving to them and they looked on with a mix of curiosity, fear, and disgust.

But truthfully, they weren't prizes either. In their overalls, and loose shirts, and scruffy, lean faces. It felt like this could be the welcome crew in hell. The women wore shapeless dresses and mostly looked old and worn out. The younger women looked pale and dull and lifeless to me. After that arrival, we went to the stockade and we hadn't seen anyone since work started a couple months ago. But this girl, who now walked closer on the trail by us, was different. First, her skin was olive, and her hair was black. I figured she was Cherokee. She stopped and watched us for a while. Because I was young and strong, I was helping set the first of the steel rails that would begin the road. Because the rails were so heavy we worked in teams of eight men, and we had songs that helped us lift and turn in tandem. It also helped pass the time and sometimes I made up new ones in my head. I kept a small pad and pencil in my pocket to write them down if I liked them. Because with the pad, it was clear to the guards and bosses I could read and figure, and this also helped, since it distinguished me from the rest of the mostly illiterate convicts.

I looked straight at her and caught her gaze as we began to sing and lift and turn the twelve foot steel rail and get it in place. She didn't downcast her eyes as most country gals would do, but looked straight back at me, and a faint smile brushed across her face when we began to sing.

Bones
Woo-wee! Look at that pretty dark girl there. Ain't seen too many mountain people yet, ain't impressed with the ones I've seen so far, but I ain't seen one like her. She a Cherokee?

Jimmy
She might be. Caught my eye, that's fer sure.

Starlight
Bones. Why they call you Bones?

Bones
Well, because I play the bones, but mostly cause I weigh about 275. 275 pounds of all muscle. Why they call you Starlight? Ain't never heard that nickname before.

Starlight
It ain't a nickname. It's my real name. I bet we could put you an ol' John Henry together and you two could dig a tunnel through rock in no time at all.

Bones
That's right, John Henry. That's who can be Brother Possum in the band. He can play the mouth harp like nobody's business.

Jimmy
Shush. You boys stop yammering. Guards looking at us. If you gonna talk, keep yer head down and keep digging.

Bones
Yes, Brother Rabbit.

Bones
They call me Bones. I was a slave and now I'm a convict with not much daylight in between. I tell stories cause somebody has to. I mean a thousand slaves live and die and nobody know em from Adam. Just live and die without a trace. Without a hello or good-bye, or even a tombstone or wooden cross to say they lived at all. Somebody needs to tell that story. Now we here to build a railroad up a mountain. Nobody will even know cause white men with money take all the credit. When I was a slave, I hear the stories-- Jack stories, and African stories bout Anassi, and Brer Rabbit stories. That's why I ain't a Christian. I went through the motions to stay out a trouble. But when they preachin and prayin, I'm thinking these bible stories just don't match up with these other stories. Something wrong and hateful bout em seem to me. Plagues, and floods, and crucifixions. Hearin' those stories makes a feller want to go out and drown em self or something. But we got the songs-- work songs, playin songs, fighting songs, praying songs, loving songs.

John Henry
Bones. Stop daydreaming and get yer sorry ass over here. We gotta move this big steel rail and get it in place. You gotta lead us in the song.

Bones
I'm comin. John Henry everybody knows you could lift that rail all by yerself if you wanted to.

John Henry
Don't want to. Now come on.

O Lord Berta Berta O Lord gal oh-ah
O Lord Berta Berta O Lord gal well

Go 'head and marry don't you wait on me oh-ah
Go 'head and marry don't you wait on me well now
Might not want you when I go free oh-ah
Might not want you when I go free well now
O Lord Berta Berta O Lord gal oh-ah
O Lord Berta Berta O Lord gal well now
Raise them up higher, let them drop on down oh-ah
Raise them up higher, let them drop on down well now
Don't know the difference when the sun go down oh-ah
Don't know the difference when the sun go down well now
Berta in Meridian and she living at ease oh-ah
Berta in Meridian and she living at ease well now
I'm on old Parchman, got to work or leave oh-ah
I'm on old Parchman, got to work or leave well now
O Lord Berta Berta O Lord gal oh-ah
O Lord Berta Berta O Lord gal well

That kinda work kill a man. Take a little break, boys. That's okay with you ain't it, guard? It's our break time. Here John Henry, I gotta story to tell ya bout Brother Possum.

Bones
Brother Possum

I ain't too smart, but I'm slow. Lawd, lawd, gonna build a train track up a mountain. Even I can beat that in a race. It'll take em years. Brother Rabbit, what do you think? You gonna trick'em. You're the smart one ain't ya. Look all these rabbits cutting, choppin, digging. Fur what? They ain't gonna get to ride on the train. Making the track that they can't ride on. Nothin smart about that.

Brother Rabbit

Lawdy, Brother Possum, listen to you gossip talk cept you talk so slow it make me fall asleep fore you get to the end of a sentence. You know what a sentence is?

Bones
Yeah. It's how long I gotta stay in this prison here.

Rabbit
Now listen up, reptile. All rabbits ain't smart like me. Some are dumb as those shovels. Some of these men are smart, some are dumb. Smart ones will survive. The dumb ones, well, some of them will survive too. Look at you. Where's the smarts in that. See that feller over there. He's smart. He's not working too hard just hard enough to look like he's working hard. He's thinking about somethin' else-- Saturday night, a dance, a gal. See those other fellers hammerin and sweatin like they diggin a hole to a sack a gold. They workin too hard for the man. They'll be dead fore the end of the season. Yes sir, not all rabbits are smart.

CHAPTER 33

Ghosts and Gossip

Elizabeth

Lord help me! Who would of thunk it? Here I got two men trying to court me at the same time, and me a widower since Calvin got killed in the war and me up in my thirties. Never had no younguns since me and Calvin were so young when he went off to war. That was about 15 years ago, and me living up here all by myself and figuring out how to farm enough, and raise chickens enough to survive. Course Preacher Andrew was a big help, and he still is. That's how I met Joseph and he started coming to visit, and I'd go down to Andrew's when they'd be playing a little music. I love the music, but I can't carry a tune in a bucket, but I could tell he was getting sweet on me, but he's a black man, not that that makes never any mind with me, and people up here don't care too much what you do. Still I'd never even seen a black man till I met Joseph.

Then this other man showed up one day. This rough, but good looking man, wanders by the cabin, and he's picking and looking at flowers, and I'm thinking what kind of crazy man just wanders up here picking flowers, so I went got my rifle. I figured it might be one of those men associated with the railroad they was building. In that case, I might just go ahead and shoot the bastard. Nobody here much wanted the damn railroad. Mainly, just the rich people and people talking about progress. I'll show'em progress. Then, he saw me, and made one step toward me, and then saw the gun. He took off his hat and looked at me in a shy way, and held up this little mushroom and said, "It's Rosemary. It'll ward off sickness." And then I recognized something about the way he talked. You ain't no man, I told'em. You a ghost. A haint. You died in the war."

Ben

No mam, I might be a ghost, but I'm a livin, breathin one. I'm Ben. Sally and Davy's Ben. I run away from that awful war just after we were introduced. You know how sometimes you meet somebody and right away--you think, something bad wrong here.

Elizabeth

Yes, I believe I do. Right now, fer example.

Ben

Well, I run away. And by the way, I was sorry to hear about yer husband. Anywho, Sally and Davy hid me up on the mountain. They's an old abandoned cabin up there. I fixed it up and stayed hid so long that I got plum used to it. Got me an old hunting dog, and named him, "Dog."

Elizabeth

I reckon that makes sense. . . But the war ended twelve years ago. You sayin you been livin up there like a hermit all this time.

Ben

Yes'um. I learned to get along fine and then eventually preferred it, and I see a few folks now and then. Sally and Davy been dead bout six years now. I got my dog and my fiddle. What more does a man need?

Elizabeth
Well, a good woman, some might say. What people you seein?
Ghost people?

Ben
Not just ghosts, but them too. I see Joseph and Andrew and Ariella
from time to time. To play music mostly. I just asked them not to tell
anybody, specially since they started building that damn railroad.

Elizabeth
And here I thought I knew everything bout everybody on this
mountain. How can I be the gossip lady if I don't know bout you?

Ben
Well, you know now. The cat's out of the bag now, but I appreciate
if you wouldn't spread it round too much.

Elizabeth
Well, I got something to say to Mr. Joseph fer keepin a secret from
me, of all people. Me and Joseph purty close, or least, I thought so.
He's gonna hear bout it. Fer the gossip part I'll just say, guess what? I
had a visit from Johnny Appleseed the other day. He came skippin by
my house, picking flowers, and showing me herbs that will heal me of
the deadly curdles, and a mushroom that will get me so high, I'll be
flying above the mountains.

Ben
Well, I didn't get much of that, but I don't skip fer nobody, missus.

Elizabeth
I know. It is just a little embellishment there, Ben. That's what
gossip is.

******

Elizabeth

Johnny Appleseed. That's what I started calling him and he started coming to visit ever once and while, and then Joseph would visit too. Neither one knew the other one was sweet on me. It was plain confusing, and I liked them both. I don't think Johnny Appleseed wanted to do no sparking. He'd been away from people a long time. He'd kiss his dog fore he'd want to kiss me, and Joseph wasn't no Casanova neither. Just three lonely people enjoying each other's company, and then here comes this damn railroad. Once me and Joseph was sitting out on the porch talking, when there came this noise like thunder, but louder and the ground shook and the porch rattled and my little jar of moonshine shook and nearly spilled. I looked at Joseph and asked, "What the hell was that?" He said, "It's the railroad. They're making a tunnel, using something called nitroglycerin. Causes an explosion that tears right through the mountain."

"Sons a bitches," I said. "Lucky they didn't spill any of this shine or I'd grab my rifle."

Joseph

There ain't no stopping the railroad. Best forget about it. Move a little deeper into the hills. They didn't have money to pay people to build it, so they convicts working. Black men mostly. Just slavery with a different name to it. Cause the train coming and there ain't no stopping it.

****

CHAPTER 34

Bones Tells a Story and Jimmy Forms a Band

The Road

They buried ten men beside the rails today. Second tunnel and there was a cave in, and it buried them alive. Ten men lost and forgotten who were already lost and forgotten. One man made a rough looking cross and put it on the side of the hill. Won't be there in five years, but the dead men will be. Dust to dust. They just another part of the road. Bout a fourth of the way finished now. Another tunnel coming up soon. The blast shakes all the hills. The animals look around and wonder why the earth is shaking like that.

Bones

Did you hear the one bout ol' Brother Lizard and Brother Rabbit? Ol Brother Rabbit taking nap in between these two iron rails they found all dug out and smooth and it made a perfect place to lay down for a nap on a hot summer day. It was curious since the steel rails ran on out a sight round the bend. Brother Rabbit ain't never seen nothing like it. Now this was down east, you know, just west of east where I come from. Now when the train come there, it come awhile back and was pretty easy except when they have to go over some of the swamp land down there. Anywho, Brother Rabbit sort of curled up on a cushion of brush, and ol Brother Lizard kinda sleeping too, but it's hard to tell when a lizard is sleeping. His eyes kinda closed but kinda open too, and he kinda standing with his claws kinda gripping the ground. He look over at Brer Rabbit and say in his kinda gravelly voice. "Did you feel that Brother Rabbit? Did you feel something?" Brother Rabbit kinda open one eye and say, "Brother Lizard, you ain't said two words in a coon's age and now you say something and wake me up. I didn't feel nothin but I heard something, but it was you sayin not much of nothin." "It was the ground a groaning. I got a good grip on the ground and now it's shaking and moaning like something wrong." "Oh go on," said Brother Rabbit. "It ain't nothing but your lizard imagination. Go back to sleep or go back awake. You know Brother Lizard, it hard to tell if you're asleep or awake." "Mark my two words. Bad thing's a coming."

"That's four words. And you know something Brother Lizard. You are an alarmist." Brer Lizard just gazed at Brother Rabbit out of those big glassy eyes and Brother Rabbit figured Brother Lizard had just gone back to sleep cause Brother Lizard had an affliction called narcolepsy. But Brother Lizard didn't know what either one of those words was. But the ground started shaking considerable enough now that even Brother Rabbit felt it, and suddenly around that turn came a big iron monster bigger than a horse barreling right toward them on those big iron rails, and they was able to jump out of the way just in time. After that monster passed, Brer Lizard stood there gripping the earth and looking unperturbed, as lizards do. Brother Rabbit was panting and finally said, "Uh, Brother Lizard. I believe you was right," and that's how Brother Lizard saved Brother Rabbit.

****

Wilson

June 6, 1877

Dearest Lou,

Now that summer is finally coming here. It really is quite beautiful. Tell me about your garden. I so miss you and the children. Tell little Joey and Matthew I have found three Cherokee spear points that I will bring home soon. Tell Mary and Abby I have purchased some corn shuck dolls and a handsome mountain dulcimer from the mountain folk here.

We are already behind schedule and Raleigh and the Republicans are pressing me, and criticizing the progress. The spring thaw so mired us at the bottom at a place called Mudcut. The clay is like quicksand and nearly swallowed up a locomotive we were using. We lost three days just trying to dig it out.

Raleigh is sending us 200 more convicts and we're building two more barracks up the mountain as we go. I have no idea when I might be able to visit. Perhaps in a month or two. I hired the young girl who has been hanging round the camp. She's smart and has a good education for people around here which isn't saying much. She a preacher's kid, but this preacher is from up north. She's a Mexican. I thought she was Cherokee. She reminds me so much of the young girl I nearly adopted during the war.

Take care and I will write again tomorrow evening.

Yours Always,

Jim

****

Jimmy

That Bones can sure tell a tale. He's got a story for everything. He's a good bit older and moves kinda slow, so they got him digging with that shovel cause he may be old and slow, but he's big and strong. Like the story he tells bout old John Henry. They got me setting some of the charges because I can read, and so they think I'm smart. That's what I get for trying to advance round here. So they give me one of the most dangerous jobs on the road. Course it's safer than the poor men digging or who go in right after the explosion cause of the cave-ins, but it's dangerous enough.

Bones is a good singer too, and can play bout anything. Play a banjo, or a mouth harp, and he can keep a crazy rhythm on his own body. He leads his crew when they using the picks or setting the rails. They setting some rails up the grade behind me today. I can hear him singing and Bones hamboning.

Well, the high sheriff

He told his deputy

Want you go out and bring me Lazarus

Well, the high sheriff

Told his deputy

I want you go out and bring me Lazarus

Bring him dead or alive,

Lawd, Lawd

Bring him dead or alive

Well the deputy he told the high sheriff

I ain't gonna mess with Lazarus

Well the deputy he told the high sheriff

Says I ain't gonna mess with Lazarus

Well he's a dangerous man

Lawd, Lawd

He's a dangerous man

Well then the high sheriff, he found Lazarus

He was hidin' in the chill of a mountain

Well the high sheriff, found Lazarus

He was hidin' in the chill of the mountain

With his head hung down

Lawd, Lawd

With his head hung down

Jimmy

It's a downright eerie sound against the echoing of the picks in the ground in these mountains. Echoes all over the place like ghost sounds. But I'm glad it's a Friday. We got kind of a regular band playing outside on Saturday night. Me and Bones and Starlight, and John Henry and a couple other guys. And Beulah been singing with us some. She was shy at first, but when she started singing, Lord! Lord! The hair on the angel's arms stood up. I have to say I'm kind of sweet on her, but we're both kinda shy, I believe. It's been so long since I been that close to a handsome woman like that. I mean, I just get all jelly-legged, and can't hardly speak a word. I start shaking inside so I just kick off another song, since that's about all I can do when I'm around her.

Beulah

By the end of the week my hands raw from washing and cleaning and scrubbing, and then washing those convict's clothes in that cold creek. That creek cold enough, without winter coming on. My hands so cracked and sore I can't close my fist. That new girl who works for boss Wilson, she saw me, saw my hands, and the next day she brought me a jar of ointment. She a mountain girl, but she don't look like those downcast, worn out looking, pale face mountain girls that I seen. No, this one is dark. I think maybe she a Cherokee, but she told me she's a Mexican from Texas. At first, I thought she was just joshin with me. What a girl from Mexico doing here? We talk a little. She's nice. Said her name was Ariella Isabella. She kind of sang the words. She's like Wilson's secretary or somethin. I can see why he hired her, ain't no mystery there. She a pretty girl. Today's Saturday, and they'll be singing and laughin and partying soon out by the barracks, and they'll build a big fire. And Jimmy and the band will play. Jimmy asked me to sing last week, but I'm too shy, but maybe I'll sing this week if they ask me.

CHAPTER 35

Let the Music Begin

Wilson, Oct. 22, 1877

Dear Louisa,

Winter will be here before I know it and we're behind schedule. We're working the convicts extra hard, so we let them blow off steam on Saturday night. Let them cut loose. No harm in that, I guess. The music's starting and it's a sight to behold. Work them to death all week, but they sure got something left for Saturday night. I don't care for music myself, or dancing, or drinking—such foolishness, but it's good for morale, just like in the army. Let them get it out of their systems that way. I'll just sit here in my office. I can see them through the window. The banjos and the drums-- you would think you were in Africa for a night. Some of the locals come down just to watch too. Some partake, and I have to tell the guards to watch out for too much mingling because the mountain folks always have a jar of moonshine on them somewhere. It reminds me of once when I was in New Orleans. I was in Vicksburg, and we took the riverboat to New Orleans. This was back before the war. On Sundays, the slaves congregated at a place they called Congo Square to play and sing. You could hear the drumming from miles away.

Starlight

My name Starlight. Least that's what they call me and that's all right by me, I guess. Dee-dee-dum. Dee dee dum. That's me playing the drum. This here is a kalimba. Some of these people call it a thumb piano cause they don't know the word "kalimba." My grannydaddy brought it all the way from Africa. My grannydaddy raised me for awhile. Anyway, til she died. I never knew my momma or daddy. Grannydaddy said the overseer got mad at my daddy and they sold'em off down the river. The river, the river flows backwards til the sea is sucked dry. Overseer told her he sold'em because he got a price he couldn't turn down. Said you'll raise the child cause you're old and not good for anything else. I got swallowed up by a fish one time, spit me out, and there I was in New Orleans. Just turned us slaves out to fend for ourselves. I always got beat up because people told me I acted like a girl. I never had no school on the plantation. I got beat up there too, and they made fun of me, and called me girl, and queer and all kind of names. I don't know. I just am who I am. Ended up in jail for not having any money or any where to go. Bah bah black sheep have you any wool? I didn't know how old I was. I told'em fifteen, and they put me in a home for colored waifs. The war was just over and the school found these abandoned musical instruments the soldier bands had left behind, and I had my kalimba and the school had a banjo and it was like I knew how to play it when I picked it up. Funny minnie haha. I ain't no good for nothing in this world, but put something musical in my hands, and it's like I've known it all along. I just hear it. I think I am a bird, but they called me Starlight cause I didn't have no other name, and I liked to sit up in a tree at night and talk to the stars and planets. Mars will talk your ear off, but Venus is quiet, and the moon, well, the moon plays the earth like I play the kalimba.

I got arrested on New Year's Eve for shooting a gun in the air. They gave me ten year's for attempted murder. I guess they thought I was trying to shoot the moon. People say I'm crazy and I talk crazy. I don't know. The stars and planets understand me, but they can't help me much, but I like sitting in a tree and talking to them.

Beulah

Starlight, Starlight come down outa that tree. Music gonna be starting. They asking for you. I might sing tonight if you come down. Sing a song just for you. I took a little sip of moonshine for courage. I believe I might just sing with you all tonight, but you need to come down outta that tree.

Bertie

Come on down from there, Starlight. I gotcha a present.

****

Andrew

God works in a wondrous and mysterious way—that such a questionable endeavor as this railroad and all the so-called progress it will bring has brought me here tonight to this odd gathering of convicts and guards, and a few local mountain people like me to this Saturday night gathering. I might say celebration except for the fact that most of the negroes are convicts who work all week for not a penny. It's a warm night for October and a large circle of convicts are gathered. Some are sitting on the ground, others standing and milling about, shouting and laughing. Some are drinking. This is the only payment they get for their hard work. One night out of seven.

There is a five or six piece band gathering and tuning in the center of the circle. They can't be heard over the roar of the hundred or so convicts. A guitar, a banjo or two, several drums of different sorts, a huge negro with a harmonica. I can't quite see with all the activity about. Around the large circle of convicts is a space of twenty feet or so where five or six guards with guns stand. Then behind them, a few feet are the mountain folks. Come down out of curiosity mostly to see so many negroes in one place, and to listen to what is about to commence.

I am here for the music. To listen to a culture of music that is as strong as it is different from all the music I studied from Scotland and Ireland. And Ariella Isabella insisted I come, although it didn't take much insistence. She's been working for Wilson and the Road for a couple months now as kind of a secretary. I think she has big plans for herself. The band is starting to play. The drums begin and the sound echoes off the mountain. The deep, earthy timbre, and the movement of people and shadows cast by the large bonfire is downright eerie. Just beyond the circle is a row of buildings near the stockade that houses the convicts. I can see a man sitting quietly, observing at a desk in what seems to be an office. I assume it is Wilson. The chief engineer of the road. Perhaps I should seek an introduction, but now the music has started. There's a certain desperation to all this. A window of ecstasy in a big house of misery.

Ariella

The drums are starting. My feet won't stand still. I love Andrew, but there's something a little stiff and reserved about him. How he intellectualizes everything. Me, I just feel the music run through me and it stirs something in me that only the music can.

Bones

One two three four. Hands on the drum. Pounding soft. Calling the air. Sound moving through the crowd. The crowd moving to the sound. My banjo frailing loud, and crackily to the beat.

Jimmy

Guitar strumming to the rhythm of the drum. Wood and string and earth and sky. One voice. Now two, and the train of music is leaving this earth for a while. Going to be going down the track that's being laid as we go.

Ariella

Feet won't stay still. Body body body. Nobody but me and the rising sound.

The Road
Don't do no harm.

Wilson
Damn crazy congo music. Don't do no harm.

Beulah
Music's started, Starlight. Come on down from that tree now. I'm
going over to dance a little bit. Maybe sing. Come on down now.
Jimmy's singing one. I can hear him.

Bertie
Come down, Starlight. I'm waiting for you. You my favorite.

Jimmy
"Cornbread and butterbeans and you across the table.'
Making love and eating beans as long as I am able."

Bones
Play those bones. Dance a little Bojangles.

Starlight
Whoo Hoo! That's nice, Master Mars. I think I might
shimmy down from this tree and shimmy over to the band.
The star waves are calling me.

Joseph
Man! This is some hot and wild stuff. Gonna have to come down
here and play in this band. I'm glad Ariella brought me. Look Lizabeth.
Look at Ariella dancing. She like a fairy. Never known anyone like her.
And man that guy playing the mouth harp. Crazy looking negro, but
that sound going right through to my soul. Give me another drink of
that shine. And then something strange happened.
"Thank ye boys fer letting us come down and listen to you fellers. . .
You play mighty good."

Bones
Yeah. Not like we have much say in anything, cept when we start
playing the music. Yes sir, reminds me of the time Brother Rabbit
started a band.

Joseph
Brother Rabbit. Man! I know I knew you from somewheres. Is that
you, Bones?

Bones
Well, dog my cats, Joseph. I ain't seen you in what, 15 or 16 years? A
brother's coon age. Goodness gracious sakes alive. So you stayed all this
time in these mountains. Regular mountain man, ain't ya?

Joseph
Yep. After my fever broke, Andrew let me stay and help out. How
bout you? Did you get caught?

Bones
Sure as I'm standing here. Cept I'm sitting on this chair right now. I
made it up to the next place, but further up in Virginia I got turned
around and lost. I tried to find some union boys to help me. I ended up
running into the whole damn union army. I ended up working fer
them in a place called Petersburg. Doing what, you ask? Digging
ditches and tunnels, of course. They was trying to dig under the rebel
lines to set off an explosion. Anywho, after the war was over I had zero
money and zero prospects, so I got put in jail fer stealing some food
from this store, and here I am. Digging ditches and making tunnels.
Moving right up sideways in this world.

Joseph
You still the same old Bones though. That's something.

Jimmy

That's something, all right, so let's play the devil right up out the ground now. You ain't holding those banjos just fer show are you?

Ben

I didn't go to the party with them. Don't go where there's that many people at one time. I'm sitting out on my porch on the ridge with my fiddle cradled in my arm like a baby. I can hear the drums start down in the valley. The music begins to echo up to me. I draw the bow soft across the strings as not to drown out the music in the distance, but to play along with it. Maybe I should have gone. Awful lonely world. Music makes it less so.

Elizabeth

They been going nonstop for a couple hours now. Ain't ever seen a party like this one. Here, but don't drink it all! We gotta start back up the mountain soon.

Jimmy

We be winding this thing down pretty soon. I seen Wilson leave his office a minute ago. He's out talking to one of the guards. I'm pretty wasted, Bones. Keep Starlight a way from that moonshine. Let's get Beulah to sing one of the old cabin songs, if she will. Let the music begin to settle things down. She been in the shine too, and dancing over there. I think she's ready.

Starlight

Beulah, Beulah, Beulah, Beulah. You said you'd sing one if I come down outta my tree. Come on now.

Bertie

Starlight right! You said you'd sing one.

Beulah
Okay, okay. One more little swig.

Jimmy
Do one of the old ones, Beulah. I've heard you in the kitchen
singing. "Run, Mourner, Run." You start us and we'll all come in
singing. Just drums, fellows.

Beulah
"Run, mourner, run. Bright angel above."

Andrew
We been listening for a couple hours. Such a wild conflagration--I've
never seen, or heard, before. The fire blazing and sweating, dancing
bodies and the shadows and the music and the horn. My God! The
devil himself ain't seen a party like this one. Even us observers are
exhausted. Then all of a sudden, everything got quiet like there was a
signal or something, and this young, pretty negro girl steps out into the
circle in front of the band and starts swaying. . .
I will need to talk to them. Some of these songs are new to me. I
need to write them down and get Ariella to memorize the melodies.

Ariella
And the drum starts kind of low, and she start singing. "Run,
Mourner run. Bright angels above." It is magical. Tears roll down my
face as if I'm watching some miracle. Then everyone begins to sway. It
feels like the planet itself is swaying to this song. Then the girl, her eyes
closed up toward the October clouds, and the cradled quarter moon.
After a couple refrains, others in the band join in. They all know the
song. Then everybody is singing the call and response.

"If I had wings. Bright angel above.
If I had wings, bright angel above.

If I had wings, bright angel above."

James Wilson can build all the railroads he wants. Make all the money he wants. But these singers with nothing but their voices and the clothes on their backs have more than any millionaire. They have these moments shared.

Bones
Whoa! Girl! Where ya learn to sing like that?

Beulah
I don't know. I just sing. I just open my mouth and the sound come.

Jimmy
That sound come outta heaven, I believe.

Beulah
Ah, you boys drunk on the moon and moonshine. I'm shy bout singing. Now I done it once and that's it.

Jimmy
Girl, you got that all wrong. The trouble with coming here and out-shining everybody, is now you part of the band. You got to sing with us now. Here let's have one more little sip of this moonshine.

Bones
Yeah, these mountain folks good fer something, I reckon.

Beulah
Okay, just one more. I ain't never done no drinking before. And John Henry, you sure can play that harmonica. That little harp and your big body, why that sound made the mountain shake.

John Henry
I thank ye, mam.

Bones
Man, that's the truth, and with John Henry we don't have to worry
bout no fights breaking out cause John here put a stop to that right
away. By the way, where is Starlight? He didn't get in the shine did he?

Jimmy
Look, he's way over there. Come on, John Henry, you better come
too.

Convict
Hey, queer boy. What's you wanta dress like a girl fer? What's ya
doing here? I'm gonna rid this camp of the likes of you.

Starlight
What's wrong with you, peckerwood? I ain't done nothin to you.

John Henry
Cuse me, gents. Is there a problem here?

Convict
Naw sir, John Henry. Just talkin.

John Henry
Make sure that's all yer doing. You call out anybody in this band
then you have to reckon with all of us.

CHAPTER 36

Something in the Air

Jimmy

After last night, I think back to when I first saw Beulah. The first thing I remember was her voice, soft and low, working in the kitchen, and me, just out of sight beyond the doorway listening. It took me back to my mother's singing and the first memory I ever had. Then, I sort of cleared my throat to let her know someone was there, and I walked in with a load of wood in my arms. She kept right on singing soft, not even looking up at me. I was going to tell her what a lovely voice she had, but I didn't, since she just kept on singing, but I looked at her so I would remember her. She was youngish, about my age, I figured, and left it at that.

Beulah

I never drunk anything like that before. Moonshine, huh? Oh, I feel awful. My head about to bust. I went down to the creek. It being Sunday, to wash up fore a whole bunch of biddy hens got down there. I hope I didn't make too big a fool last night. I know I sang, and everything got quiet and my heart was beating out of my chest. I just have to avoid everybody today. Do my chores. Stay by myself. I think I had fun though. Maybe too much fun, but I sure paying for it now. As I'm walking back up to the boxcars and stockade, I hear a rustle in a maple tree and there's Starlight back up in his tree. Sitting there, and who is up in the tree with him but Bertie.

Starlight
Well, girl, girl, girl. You shore did sing, sing, sing last night. You had'em dancing and laughing and crying and shaking, and singing, all at the same time. You're a star, girl. Who taught you to sing like that? I sang with ya after a time. It was plum beautiful. Makes me glad I'm just a crazy son of a bitch. All these birds flying in today. They heard about you too. They jealous. Be careful. They might buzz ya. Out singing the birds. Land's sake!

Bertie
It true, Beulah. You are beautiful.

Beulah
Bertie what you doing up there with Starlight. You startin to be with the wrong crowd. You be getting into trouble.

Bertie
Starlight the right kind of people. I'll be alright.

****

Jimmy
I can't stop thinking bout her. Glad it's Sunday. Just think about her all day. Get her to sing with me. I guess singing the closest think to sex there is. Maybe closer. I don't know. They put me in jail fore I ever got a chance with a woman. Maybe I fall in love with her cept this ain't no place to fall in love. They a good bit of pairing off around here, but the girls awful outnumbered. Course Beulah ain't like that. She shy like me. Keeps to herself. Who knew she could sing like that, but this ain't no place to fall in love. Working and sweating and stinking. Taking a bath once a week or so in that cold creek. Maybe got soap, maybe not. Sleeping in a stockade with a bunch of other men crammed in there

tight. They treat us like animals, but I can't stop thinking bout her. Maybe talk to her bout singing later. Just talking. Can't be no harm in that.

Wilson

Well, there isn't any harm in it as I see it. Let'em blow off steam. I sat in my office going over drawings and maps over the next phase of the road. We're getting close to halfway, but the really hard part is coming. We got three more tunnels to do in this phase. It's going to slow us down considerably. Let'em party. Let'em thank me for letting them. It's alright. I'm just a good soldier. I don't care much for music myself. I'd look up from my maps out at the music and the dancing. My eyes always fell on Ariella Isabella. Her face glowing in the light of the fire, moving with the music, standing next to an older man, about the same age as me. I guess that's the preacher she keeps talking about. She's a special child. I go back to my maps, but my eyes keep looking up at her. Discipline, man.

I keep thinking she's the little girl I almost adopted. But the army left the Shenandoah, and I never went back. The memory enshrined some place in my soul. Crystalized. Why? Something I missed? Something unexplainable. She is not the same girl. I should write my wife a letter right now.

Wilson

Dearest Lou,

I was thinking about our wedding the other day. How strange and faraway it seems, but know I love you my dear and the children. I haven't had a letter from you in a week. I hope all is well there. Do you remember how we kissed at the end of the ceremony? Then the war, and I had to leave you, and you were pregnant with our first child. Why does duty constantly pull me away from you? I promise when this is finished I'll come home to be with you for a long spell.

The road continues. We finished the trestle at Long View and now comes the tunnels. There is a new product called Nobel Blasting Oil that is more powerful and cheaper than gunpowder. You mix it into a mash and we are learning how to use it here. Don't worry, I'll be safe, but it will help speed up our progress.

Kiss the children for me and write me when you get the chance. I miss you.

Yours Always,

Jim

****

Beulah

That Jimmy, he handsome, and can play and sing. I remember him looking at me in the kitchen that day I was singing. I knew he was watching me, but I pretended I didn't notice, but I felt his eyes. We ain't never talked much. You know, teased around. He's the one kept asking me to sing with'em. After I had a drink or two of that moonshine, we started making eyes at each other. He sweet on me, I think, but it's hard living and working in a place like this.

Bertie

Ain't it funny. His name Starlight and you drank moonshine. Starlight, moonshine.

Beulah

Gal, you listening to me? I ain't never been with a man that way. That white man tried one time, but I screamed and bit him on the arm, and kicked him in the balls, and then I get arrested cause the wife jealous. Accuse me of stealing. All the work we have to do for these people, and we don't even get to live, so thinking bout Jimmy makes the time go by a little sweeter. And the music, I all the time singing to myself.

Bertie
Starlight say when you singing to yourself you really singing to the stars that hear you better than people and they sing back.

Beulah
Poor Starlight. I wonder how he got that name? Sitting in trees, I guess. I wonder if anybody ever love him? When I think of him, I don't feel so sorry for myself, but he has music too, but there's something wild and desperate about it. You be careful. Starlight liable to bring trouble down on his head.

Bertie
Starlight say my name Bertie cause I'm meant to be a bird. But I don't much like climbing up in trees cause I'm afraid of falling. He says that cause I'm supposed to be flying.

CHAPTER 37

Ben and Ariella

Ben

The first thing I remember was her voice. I live alone far up on the mountain above the valley. I guess I'm a hermit cause I don't care to mingle with the human race. Cept for Joseph and a few of the music fellers. That's why I didn't go down to the party the other night. All that noise and commotion. I start having flashbacks of being in the war and I have to skedaddle.

So I'm on my porch playing my fiddle. I'm playing one of the old ballads from the old country. I call it "Two Sisters," but it goes by lots of names. Bout two sisters who love the same man, and one pushes the other into the river and she drowns. Her body floats down the river and comes to rest in the rushes, and a fiddler finds her bones and hair, and makes a fiddle out of her. Real cheery. Those old ballads knew what the human race was, and it ain't changing.

Ariella Isabella

The first thing I heard was a fiddle playing deep and mournful up on the ridge. It vibrated the air and rose above the trees like a soft wind, so I followed the sound up the winding rocky trail to a cabin. I knew who lived there but was informed to stay away unless I wanted my head bitten off, but the music was irresistible. Without knowing anything about the player, I knew from the playing, here was a sweet, kind human. Well, people can be just as fake, and lie, and cheat ya, and pretend to be something they ain't with their actions and words, but you can't fake good playing, not that good, and besides, I knew the song. Andrew had taught it to me. So the closer I got to the cabin, I began to sing the melody along with the fiddle.

Ben

So I'm playing the song, slow and wistful. The birds are answering just below the cabins in the oaks and poplars, and I'm soaking in the beauty of the morning like I always do. They'll be wood to chop, and work to do, chickens to tend to, and beans to cook, but I always play the fiddle early in the morning. First thing after I build a fire and make the coffee. When you live alone, you have to learn to communicate with things around you--the birds, the trees, the flowers and weeds.

Then I hear something that's not a bird, but it sounds like singing. Maybe the wind, up through the rhododendron, but no, it's singing, singing the song I'm playing. "That's it, I've lost my mind living by myself like they said I would." The singing gets closer and a girl emerges from the trail. She sings the words,

> "He made a fiddle bow of her long yellow hair.
> Oh the wind and rain.
> He made a fiddle bow of her long yellow hair.
> Oh the dreadful wind and rain."

She is small, lithe, like a fairy. She has the blackest black hair I'd ever seen, and dark eyes that were wide and seemed to take in the whole world. I knew who she was.

"He made fiddle screws from her little fingers bones. . ."

She sang ghost beautiful. The words lingering on the air like wisps of smoke. I knew who she was. This is the girl, Andrew, the preacher man had adopted and brought to the mountain. I only went down to the settlement once ever six weeks, or so, to get what I couldn't get, make, or grow here. Take my fiddle with me and play with Joseph. Don't talk to anyone really, but a story like that one. A yankee abolitionist adopts a girl from Mexico and brings her to live up here. Well, that story gonna get told, and twisted round something awful. People mind their own business up here, but they talk.

"The only tune that fiddle would play.
Is oh the wind and the rain.
The only tune that fiddle would play,
Is oh the dreadful wind and rain.

Arieilla
"You play mighty fine. I ain't heard anyone play that nice and I love that song, don't you? I'm sorry just to come up here like this. I know you don't like people, but I ain't people exactly. Not like most people, I reckon. I had to follow the sound of your fiddle. You might not talk much. Your fiddle talks for you."

Ben
"Well, I have to say, you took me by surprise. Last person to walk up this trail was some years ago. You sing real nice too. You the preacher's girl, ain't ya?"

Ariella
"Yes sir, my name is Ariella Isabella. You might make up a fiddle tune to go with my name. I always think of my name is like a line of music, but don't make it mournful and as sad as the song you was doing. Something lively and joyful."

Ben
"Well, I'll think on that a while. Make no promises."

Ariella
"You know Joseph. Don't ya? Andrew helped Joseph a long time ago. Joseph picks with us sometimes. We went down to the camp where they building the railroad. They hundreds of negroes and they a big music and dance party Saturday night. It was something else. Nothing like I seen before."

Ben
"Yeah. I heard it. Them drums echo all up out of the valley. I ain't much for big gatherings like that."

Ariella
"Andrew talking bout going back next Saturday and taking our instruments. He's real interested in all kinds of music. And I'm a song catcher."

Ben
"A song catcher? I know a world full of songs."

Ariella
"Andrew keeps a book of songs. He's an educated man. He writes them down. Joseph helps him. They go round the mountain some when he ain't preaching, and writes em down. Makes squiggly marks on lines. Don't get me wrong. He sings too. He loves the music."

Ben
"Yeah. Joseph, bout the only person i talk to. He's a good man."

Ariella
"You should come down to our cabin when Joseph is there and play with us. We need a good fiddle player, and it sounds like you're the best in these parts."

Ben

"Birds think so anyway. The trees still uncertain about it. They hear a lot good fiddle players. Mostly buried ones, but the trees still hear em. I might ponder visiting. I ain't totally anti-social. I visit the widow, Elizabeth, sometimes. I talk a little, when I can get a word in. She likes to talk."

Ariella

"That's the truth. She comes with Joseph sometimes. I think Joseph is sweet on her a little. Well, I gotta be getting back and I didn't mean to interrupt your playing. I bet you're done tuckered out from talking so much to me."

Ben

"Exhausted, but I'm glad you followed the song and sang. I think you are one of the birds is all. I'll think about what you said."

Ariella

"A Goldfinch or Mountain Whippoorwill? I thank ye for the compliment."

Ben

And then she was gone. Singing as she went. I followed her voice down the trail. I ran my fiddle bow over the strings and droned to her fading melody. I took a breath of the sweet morning air and smiled at this fairy visitation. What just happened here?"

CHAPTER 38

Love and Father Time

Bones
Well, you know Ol Brother Rabbit got curious bout love. Ain't no
surprise is it? Rabbit live a life running round tricking others, out-
smarting others, getting into fixes, getting out of fixes. Having a high
good ol' time all the time. Comes a time though when Brother Rabbit
started losing a little hop out of his step. Ain't no tricking Father Time.

Starlight
Nope, ain't no tricking father time. See those three stars in a row.
They say that's Orion's Belt. Somebody just made that up.

Bones
So Brother Rabbit start thinking bout settlin down a little bit, and
Brother Fox see an opportunity. To get back at em for that old tar baby
trick, he sculpted the likeness of a female rabbit that was the spittin
image of a real one. Brother Rabbit come along, and he start flirtin like
he do, and she don't speak or acknowledge Brother Rabbit in any way.

Starlight
Those three stars is me, you and Jimmy. I can make stuff up too.
Ain't no belt. Only belt I know is the one they use to beat me with.

Bones
You can see right away he's smitten and her ignoring him made him fall in love with her right on the spot. He keep saying, " Why you the prettiest thing I ever seen, Miss Rabbit, how come you don't want to talk to me? I'm the smartest, handsomest rabbit in all these parts."

Starlight
Those three stars, you know, they point to the brightest star in all the heavens. The ones we can see anyway. There's lots we don't see.

Bones
That's when Brother Fox could not resist and since he was hiding behind a tree nearby. He squealed in his best high pitch voice. He said "Oh Brother Rabbit. You too old. I need a young stud rabbit. You bout ready to be put out in the meadow." Well, you could see this made ol Brer Rabbit so mad that he hopped off in a huff. He hopped off and leaped up in the air just to show that uppity cow who was too old. He'd be back, he thought to himself, just gotta do a few pushups. Get back in shape.

Starlight
That's a mighty amusing story, Bones. You the best at making things up.

Bones
Whatcha mean, Starlight? Every word is true. True as your stars up there, and I'm not even sure you was listening. What star is that pale one, kinda green?

Starlight
That ain't no star. That's Mars and he ain't talking to me right now. And yeah, I was listening. You talking bout Brother Rabbit getting married.

Bones

Yeah, something like that. Ain't nobody in this hellhole getting married, but I think Jimmy is sweet on Beulah. It plain they kinda go together. Like them stars you talkin bout.

****

Joseph

That sure was a good time last night, wasn't it, Elizabeth? I saw you cutting a rug out there in the circle.

Elizabeth

You won't doing so bad yourself. You buck dancing out there like you a kid.

Joseph

Made me feel like a kid. Ain't never been round so many people before, especially my own. They maybe was fifty of us slaves back at the Carson House. We had a shindig or two on Saturdays, but nothing resemblin last night.

Elizabeth

Those poor men. Some of'em look pretty rough. I hear bout three or four die everyday in some sort of accident building the damn railroad, and the explosions shaking the ground and scaring all the livestock. My hens ain't laying like they should. I think it's that damn nitroglycerin, or whatever they call it. And I hear they're starting on another tunnel.

Joseph

How you hear that?

Elizabeth

Ariella Isabella tell me. She works down there for the main man.
You saw him down there in his office while everybody out partying.
And he sitting in there looking all stern and figuring new ways to blow
up mountains, I reckon. But Ariella come up here every week or so to
pick up some eggs and such. That's one girl that can't be still. She
wants to leave the mountain and make something of herself. Good
luck with that, I say.

Joseph

Well, you're no slouch. Running this little farm with the chickens
and your cows and corn patch, and cooking all the time, and now that I
seen you dancing. You quite the spry young thing, Elizabeth.

Elizabeth

You shut your mouth, Joseph Carson. I couldn't do it without you coming
    up here and helping me out. You and Ben. I'm old, old. Up
near 35 or thereabouts, but don't go spreading that around, and
you two playing your music on the porch. Keeps a body young.
That and Ginseng. You a good sang picker, too. You can find it
when nobody else can.

Joseph

Oh, I learned back at the Carson House when I was younger. A
Cherokee boy taught me how to find it. We had to keep ol man Carson
supplied with it. He was quite the rounder, you know, but he was a lot
of people's daddy down at the slave cabins. A few light skinned slaves
got born there, and I think the older the old man got the more trouble
he had, you know, and he swore Ginseng revitalized him, if you know
what I mean.

Elizabeth
Joseph Carson, you going to go embarrass me talking like that.
Making me blush.

Joseph
Elizabeth, you quite a handsome woman when you blush.

Elizabeth
You go on now. Talking like that. How come your last name
Carson? You took his name. Maybe he is your daddy.

Joseph
Naw, That ain't the reason. Didn't have a last name and figured I
needed one if anybody asked. Seems I's ahead of my time cause when
they freed Carson's slaves they all took his name. I gotta a whole lot of
relatives down the mountain it seems.

Elizabeth
"I bet you courted a lot of women back there when you were
younger. You being the Sang Picker and all, and a musician. Women
always going after the music makers."

Joseph
"Nah. I's awful young when I ran away, and bashful. Besides, I lack
experience in those things and here I am closer to 50. That's no spring
chicken, but don't you go spreadin that around. We both know you a
bit of a talker. . . Matter of fact, I wouldn't mind if we might court a
little bit. We already working together, and visiting and talking. Seems
to me we already sliding in that direction a little bit."

Elizabeth
"Land's sake, Joseph! You trying to turn me every shade of red there
is, but well, you do have a point and I might consider it, but we gotta
go slow."

CHAPTER 39

The Kiss

Jimmy
"You comin Saturday to the party?"

Beulah
"Where else I be going? To the Old Fort Ball?"

Jimmy
To the what?

Beulah
I'm just going on with you. I'll be there.

Jimmy
I wasn't sure. You been kind of stand-offish here lately.

Beulah
Standoffish! What's you talking bout? Ain't like none of us gotta any time during the week, and well, I mighta drunk a little too much of that moonshine. Hope I didn't make a fool.

Jimmy
Beulah Dean, what you talkin bout? You had the whole
place buzzin with excitement. You're a star, girl. Only problem
is they be expectin it now.

Beulah
I ain't no star.

Jimmy
Yeah you is.

Beulah
Star of the prison camp. Captive audience, I guess.

Jimmy
You a star to me. I ain't never heard anyone sing like that. It
reminded me of my momma.

Beulah
Your momma? Anything else bout me remind you of your
momma?

Jimmy
No, just the opposite, I reckon. What I be thinking bout when I
think of you? Well, I wouldn't be thinkin bout my momma.

Beulah
Well, I'd love to stand here and chit chat all day, but I got about a
ton of taters to boil.

Jimmy
When I get back tonight, I be helping setting charges for the next
tunnel, so it won't be too late. Why don't you meet me by the big oak

tree over by the creek and we can practice a little bit. I got some ideas bout Saturday.

Beulah
I bet you do. You and your momma.

Jimmy
Now, Beulah. Quit going on with me. You know what I mean. Sing a little bit.

Beulah
"Won't have much time but okay. . . " *(Jimmy exits.)*
My, my, that's a kind, handsome man there. Well, taters. I guess you waiting to be peeled.

****

Bones
Man, Jimmy. I'm dead dog tired. I ain't never dug so much. Damn tunnel. Thanks fer gettin me on your crew there. Teaching me a little bout the blasting powder. The nitro. . . Wilson seemed okay with it.

Jimmy
Nitroglycerin.

Bones
Yeah. I know a little bit bout using it. I just can't say it. Where ya going, Jimmy?

Jimmy
Beulah coming to sing a little bit.

Bones
You as lucky and clever a soul as Brother Rabbit.

Bones
Hey, Beulah, Nitro Jimmy asked me to come with ya all, but I said I
couldn't.

Beulah
What you talkin bout, Bones?

Jimmy
He don't know. . . Bye, Bones. Here, I got my guitar. Let's go. The
moon up. We can see well enough since that tree out in the field a bit.

Beulah
You blow up any mountains today?

Jimmy
Tomorrow. . . You'll hear it. I'm just their helper, their mule, but a
smart mule though. I help captain with the charge. Not exactly the
safest job in the world, but safer than the men who have to go in after
the explosion. I got Bones on my crew.

Beulah
You be careful out there. Don't want to lose the guitar man. If you
die up there, can I have your guitar? I always wanted to learn to play,
but never had enough money to get one.

Jimmy
You a funny girl, ain't you, Beulah? I'll tell you what I'll do. You sit
there on that rock and we'll sing a few tunes. Quiet now. We don't
want to attract no crowd. Course the men so tired they won't be stir-
ring, but somebody said your singing could raise the dead and there's a
graveyard up the way there, so don't sing too loud. Then, I'll teach you
a few chords, but now that's pretty valuable information, so I'll need a
little compensation, I think they call it.

Beulah
You pretty funny yourself. I ain't got no money.

Jimmy
"Well, I'll tell you what'll I do. I'll give you a little guitar lesson for a kiss."
I hope you don't think I'm too forward, and I do it right? I hate to admit it but I ain't never kissed anyone. (*They kiss.*)

Beulah
So it's payment in advance, I see. How about if I pay you a month in advance? (*Beulah kisses Jimmy.*)

Jimmy
I must done it part way right to get a kiss back like that! That a hundred dollar kiss, so I reckon I owe you some change.

Beulah
Go on now! We better start singing fore you get us in trouble.

CHAPTER 40

Fever and Voodoo

Ariella

It was Sunday when I started feeling strange. It was a certain dizziness like I was flying, and it seemed I had a fever. Also, I noticed a rash on my elbow that began to spread to my legs. There was an outbreak of a fever among the convicts, so I knew I had to tell Andrew right away.

Andrew

Dear Waldo,

It has been fifteen years or more since I last saw you, and although I did not attempt to correspond I wanted you to know you have often been in my thoughts. After the death of my wife, Ellen, I left Concord never to return. I moved to the mountains of North Carolina where I helped runaway slaves much like my father-in-law did many years ago. It is a topic I was introduced to in your house at one of your gatherings.

I adopted an orphan Mexican child who had been brought to the Quakers in Salem, and I have raised her as my own. She was four or five when I adopted her, and something in her eyes and spirit reminded me of my Ellen. Now that she is seventeen, she has blossomed into a smart and beautiful woman all her own, although I can't help but see my deceased wife in her from time to time.

I am writing now because she has contracted a fever, Scarlet Fever, the same fever that took Ellen, and your first son. I have a book of your essays I am reading to her in hopes it soothes the fever. There is not much else to do. The first snow came about a week ago and it is snowing again. The only doctor is down in the small settlement of Old Fort, and he is busy with an outbreak there, and he is often drunk and unreliable anyway. Luckily, I have a couple neighbors who are steeped in natural remedies-- herbs and teas. I am sure you would have an interest in these.

Yours always,

Andrew

Elizabeth

One teaspoon of yarrow, one of angelica, one of rosemary, one of elderberry, mixed in a tea will help hold the fever. Give her water to keep her hydrated, but let the fever run its course. It will help kill the sickness inside her. Joseph is bringing over some salve to put on her rashes. He learned to make it when he was a slave at the Carson House. Our poor dear Ariella. Our poor brave girl. It's going to be a long night.

Joseph

Here Elizabeth, rub this salve on the places the rashes are. I'm going to play the banjo over in the corner. Andrew is going to read his Mr. Emerson to her. It will help sooth her spirit.

Andrew

What's in this salve? It stinks to high heaven. I hope it helps. The smell could surely raise the dead.

Joseph

I can't tell ya. But when I was a young boy, my momma, Kadella, made it. Said she learned it from her momma in Africa. Ever so often there was an outbreak in the slave quarters, and she was the doctor. I saw it work then. She taught me, and I might teach Elizabeth sometime since she knows so much about the mountain herbs. It has to be handed down that way. Now get to rubbing because there's no time to spare. If she makes it through the night, she might have a chance. The salve has to have time to settle into her skin.

Andrew

I trust you, Joseph. May God help her.

Joseph

That's why he put the plants here. Person has to know and respect how to use'em. That's what Kadella taught me. Now, see her moanin and rockin. She's havin fever dreams and visions.

Ariella

Ariella Isabella that is not your name. I am your father swimming, swimming across the river to you. You are Rosa. Red with the death. Come and join me in my drowning. Come be with me. Ariella Isabella is a song, and a dream, and a song and a dream always end. Wake up to your death, Rosa and come be with me.

Andrew

"To go into solitude, a man needs to retire as much from his chamber as from society. I am not solitary whilst I read and write, though nobody is with me. But if a man would be alone, let him look at the stars. The rays that come from those heavenly worlds, will separate between him and what he touches. One might think the atmosphere was made transparent with this design, to give man, in the heavenly bodies, the perpetual presence of the sublime."

Ariella

Father oh father. My name is Ariella Isabella. It sings and when it sings it makes me who I am. If I am Rosa, then I am drowning with you, father. You named me twice. You named me Rosa when I was a baby, but I forgot and Rosa died, but you named me in a dream. You called me Ariella Isabella. Then you disappeared beneath the current.

Come Rosa. Come to me in my dream, in your dream. Death is singing.

Elizabeth
What's she saying?

Andrew
She's delirious with the fever.

Joseph
"You are my sunshine. My only sunshine.
You make me happy when I am gray.
You'll never know dear how much I love you.
So please don't take my sunshine away."
Keep reading Andrew. We are entering her dream. Elizabeth keep
applying the salve.

Andrew
There I feel that nothing can befall me in life,— no disgrace, no
calamity, (leaving me my eyes,) which nature cannot repair. Standing
on the bare ground, — my head bathed by the blithe air, and uplifted
into infinite space, — all mean egotism vanishes. I become a transparent eye-ball; I am nothing; I see all; the currents of the Universal
Being circulate through me; I am part or particle of God.

Joseph
"You are my sunshine my only sunshine."

Ariella
I am so tired, father, and want to sleep.
Oh Rosa, you wanted to see the world. But the world is a cruel, heart-
less place. Full of pain and anguish. I am here waiting for you. Drown-
ing forever in the peace of forgetting, forgetting. Come Rosa.

*No. You are Ariella Isabella. A fairy spirit floating above the world.
Hear the music. Hear the voices.*

Joseph
"You make me happy when skies are gray."

Andrew

Dear Waldo,

I read your essay, "To Nature" to Ariella as her fever caused her to
thrash about and call out. But as I read, she began to calm and breathe a
little more peacefully. I remember the first time I read this to Ellen and
how thrilled we were. It was the philosophy we had been searching for
and we were thrilled we were going to hear you speak.

Elizabeth
Andrew, Joseph, wake up! You must have dozed off. Her breathing
is getting shallower and more raspy. I'm afraid we're losing her.

Andrew
What? Oh, Ariella don't leave us, child.

Joseph
She's struggling to breathe. Hang on, girl. Here, Lizabeth. Dab
some of the salve on her chest. It'll help her breathe. I'm going down to
my cabin. I'll be back in an hour.

Elizabeth
Joseph Carson, there's a foot of snow out there, and it still coming
down. What's ya going for?

Joseph
I'll be back.

Elizabeth
Poor dear girl. I watched the life draining out of her just as the morning light was coming in the window. Andrew sitting beside her holding her hand. Head bent, praying. We all had seen enough of death, but seems death had not seen enough of us. Andrew had an old clock on his mantle that ticked, and when the room got silent, it sounded like a heart beating. And with every tick it seemed Ariella's breathing got fainter and fainter until it stopped. We sat there for what seemed like a long time as the clock kept on ticking, ticking. Andrew bent his head down to Ariella's parched lips. I could almost see her spirit rising from her wasted little body. I listened for Joseph to come stomping the snow off his boots outside the door.
"She's gone, Andrew. Angel done come and got her."

Andrew
No. Not yet. Here, I'll hold the mirror up to her lips. See, look, there's a faint film of mist. See it.

Eliz
That's your own breath, Andrew. Move back a little. . . She's gone. Listen, there's Joseph.

Joseph
There's two feet of snow down in the hollar. Thought a drift was going to swaller me up. Look I found something my momma gave to me years ago.

Eliz
It's too late, Joseph. She's gone. She stop breathing a few minutes back.

Joseph
You see this little vial? You know, my momma learned medicine in
Africa from her mother. I saw her use this on a few people who white
doctors said was dead. I ain't sayin it will work on Ariella, and I've had
it for more than twenty years with no cause to use it, but it worth a try.

Andrew
I don't know, Joseph. Let her rest. It's over. I'm not sure how I feel
about the black arts.

Joseph
Black arts, nothin. It just a different kind of human medicine that
grow natural that white people don't understand. Here, I'll place just
three drops on her lips here. She's at death's door but she ain't crossed
over yet. There's plants and animals can go into a place between life
and death for quite a while, and can go either way. Humans can do that
too.

Elizabeth
Now what?

Joseph
We wait. And we think good thoughts to help pull her back. She
ain't ready to die. That child got too much life in her. She a handful.
Death don't want her yet. She'd drive him crazy.

Eliz
Talking bout crazy. Andrew, your clock ticks like it some kind a
bomb bout to go off.

Andrew
How long do we wait? Look how it is snowing.

Joseph

Sometimes, it's a way back to the living. Here hold that mirror up to her lips.

Andrew

Nothing, Joseph. I'm afraid this is futile.

Joseph

Wait. Hold it up again. Here let me. . . Look. There's a misting. She breathing, barely, but she breathing. Look Lizabeth. See it. See it.

Elizabeth

Yes! Yes! Look, Andrew. She breathing. I'll get the washcloth. Keep her cool. Thank the Lord, and your Momma's voodoo.

Joseph

It ain't voodoo, Lizabeth. It from the love of the earth.

Andrew

Thank you, Joseph. But it's not over yet. She's got a long way to go.

Elizabeth

She's going to make it, Andrew. My old mountain bones tell me.

****

Beulah

Starlight, Starlight, you up in that tree. I'm awful sorry, but our Bertie's dead. She died last night of the fever.

Starlight

I know it. This world too mean fer Bertie.

Beulah
How you know she dead?

Star
Little bird told me. I saw her spirit fly up. At first, she a bird. Her spirit came and sat with me fer the shortest of times. Shorter than life. Shorter than death. Then she flew up and up and now she a star.

Beulah
I'm sorry Starlight. I sat with her and held her hand. The doctor too busy with the sick men who they need more. Course, he too drunk then to help her anyway. I didn't want his filthy hands on her. She died peaceful.

Starlight
The night sky awful bright in the last dark of morning. She up there. See. Just past ol stuck up Mars. See that faint dot. It a star I never seen before. That Bertie. She up there.

CHAPTER 41

Red is the Rose

Andrew

March 17, 1878

Dear Ellen,

I am writing to you today to say after all these years I still miss you and love you. You died when you were pregnant with our first and only child. It is difficult to justify the ways of God to man. I have not seen your grave in many years, but often write to your father to place a garland of roses on your grave. It is your birthday today, and I dream what you would look like, and how you would feel if you were here. But the irony is I never would have left that life had you not died of the fever. That life was too good and your sweet presence would have just enriched that. So I have you to thank in a strange way for this strange life I have pursued. There is a lot of music here and you would have loved it. You would love the people and their honest closeness to this earth, and Ariella Isabella has your spirit. I knew that as quickly as I saw here. Your spirit inhabits her and she is an angel on this earth.

Ben

I keep listening for her voice through the trees. All through November and December and then the big snows came, and I hunkered down for the long winter. It is now March, and the spring, at last, spring is showing signs of returning, but Ariella did not return. But the winter was difficult, and her cabin is two miles away down the steep trail. I haven't seen another person in nearly five months. Just me and Dog here. I like to talk outloud to myself. I think Dog likes it too. He turns his head as if to listen, and he gives me good advice by not speaking. I've kept busy making things. I built a dulcimer out of walnut, and I built a small shed, and started a fiddle. I made it through the winter, but I have to go down into the settlement soon for I am out of just about everything.

Now, I'm out on my porch playing a tune I promised to write for Ariella Isabella. It's a lively tune in a minor key. I tried to give it a little Mexican feel, but I don't know. Dog doesn't like it much, but he's not a fan of the fiddle. When I start to play, he gives me that look and slinks off the porch, and away around back of the cabin. He has his business. I have mine. I lose myself in the tune when suddenly, I hear Ariella, or maybe I imagine I hear her. No! it is her!

And then there she is at the bottom of the steps. She smiles as if she was just here yesterday, and not five months ago.

Ariella

I tried to match the tune, but I ain't familiar with it. Pretty though. What is it?

Ben

I call it Ariella Isabella. It's the tune I wrote for you.

Isabella
Land's sake! I forgot about that. My very own tune. And it's
my birthday too. March 17, 1878. Eighteen today.

Ben
Happy birthday, girl. Funny. You don't look Irish.

Isabella
You ever hear of the Black Irish? Survivors of the Spanish
Armada that washed up on the Irish Coast.

Ben
Can't say I have. I must of been absent from school that
day.

Isabella
Well, I ain't that, but I figure all the Irish tunes Andrew
taught me, and being born on St. Patrick's Day makes me
honorary Irish.

Ben
Come up and set a spell. First warm spring day since old
man winter nearly killed us this time. I ain't been off the place,
but I made something I wanna show you, and you can sing
some of those Irish songs you talking about.

Isabella
Yep, nearly killed us that's for shore.

Ben
What's you mean? You shore look a little puny. You lost
weight.

Isabella

Had a fever. Andrew said I actually stopped breathing for a
few minutes. Joseph brought me back from the dead, I reckon.

Ben

I'm sorry, Ariella. But you okay now?

Ariella

Fit as a fiddle. It back in January during that second big
snow. I'm rested up. Ready to sing. Strum a chord on that
dulcimer. Let me hear it. It shore is beautiful.

Ben

I saw a few made and figured I could do it. It's easy to play.
You just strum it like this, and it makes a chord. You know the
"Red, Red Rose."

Isabella

It's beautiful. I can sing my heart out, but can't play no
instrument. Haven't seen many of these lately. I'm going down
to the office. Those drums drown out an instrument like that.

Ben

They still having the parties?

Isabella

Nah, not since the big snow. Least not that we've gone too.
I'm still working though. Work got stalled pretty good, but I'm
learning to do a lot paperwork and such. Get me a good job
one of these days in Raleigh maybe, or Asheville, but yeah.
Let's sing. I know that song.

Ben

I thought maybe you got yourself a beau or something.
Comely girl like you. Must be a lot of the boys looking your
way.

Isabella

Ben, how many young men you seen round here? All the
young boys pushing up daisies cause of the war. You know
that. Anyway I ain't got time for that. Working and all. That's
why they using convicts to build the road, cause all the boys
dead or missing arms and legs. Course the convicts work for
free. That's another reason.

Red is the rose by yonder garden grows
And fair is the lily of the valley
Clear is the water that flows from the Boyne
But my love is fairer than any.
T'was down by Killarney's green woods that we strayed
And the moon and the stars they were shining
The moon shone its rays on her locks of golden hair
And she swore she'd be my love forever.
Red is the Rose by yonder garden grows
And fair is the lily of the valley
Clear is the water that flows from the Boyne
But my love is fairer than any.
It's not for the parting that my sister pains
It's not for the grief of my mother
It is all for the loss of my bonnie Irish lass
That my heart is breaking forever.
Red is the Rose by yonder garden grows
And fair is the lily of the valley.

Ben
That's about a pretty a version that I ever heard. Look, even Dog liked it, and he's pretty particular when it comes to music. He don't mind the dulcimer though. Look, the birds are leaning in.

Isabella
Oh, go on. But thank ye kindly, Dog. You play nice, Ben, and it's such beautiful wood.

Ben
It Walnut. I cut it and shaved it myself. Took me part of the winter working in the evenings. You know you forget what loneliness is when you live by yourself for so long. You don't get lonely so much, but hearing you sing that song, well, it made me feel lonely and happy and sad at the same time.

Isabella
Yeah, those songs do that. Let's sing another. A happier one this time.

Ben
Well, they're Irish, so they ain't too many of those.

Isabella
Look, the sun getting a little low. We sung the day plum dry. I better go. Those couple miles ain't gonna walk themselves, but I'll be back. I won't wait five months this time, and we'll go down to the parties with the weather breaking and all.

Ben
Here, I gotta a birthday present for you. Close your eyes.

Isabella
Okay. What is it?

Ben
Here, it's the dulcimer. I made it for you.

Isabella
It's beautiful. It's the best gift. Thank you. Can I hug your neck?
Will you show me how to play it? Well, that was like hugging a stone.
Here, put your arm around me, on my back. That's better. Pretend
you're holding a flower and not a porcupine.

Ben
Been a long spell since I hugged anybody. So I thank ye. Here, it's a
simple instrument. Just strum it, and you've got a chord. You'll pick it
up in no time, and again, thank you for your gift to me.

Isabella
Gift? What gift?

Ben
The hug you just gave me.

Isabella
That wasn't the gift. This is. (*she kisses him*) This is called kissing.
It's like hugging with your lips. There. Now that's a proper thank you.

Ben
I've never been kissed. Not like that, ever. I never know much what
to say. Now I doubly don't know what to say.

Isabella

Thank you will do. I have to get back now. Thank you, Ben. I'll bring it back in a day or so. Maybe you'll come down to the party with us Saturday.

Ben

"Maybe. If I get done hugging flowers instead of porcupines.

CHAPTER 42

The Walk Back Home

Joseph
Some party won't it? I've missed these gatherings. Keeps the blood
stirred up til the next one.

Elizabeth
Your moonshine don't hurt anything neither.

Joseph
Keeps the energy up, I'd say, especially on a cool night like this one.
You folks ready to head back up the mountain. We got a good moon up
there to guide us. Shore was nice to have you here, Ben. That fiddle just
cuts through everything, even the drums.

Ben
Thank ye, Joseph. It was fun. I ain't never played with so many
people and people dancing. My fiddle be jealous now. Seems like it likes
people a bit more than I do.

Isabella
Well, if we can't drag you out of your hermit ways maybe the fiddle
will.

Ben
You and that girl singing together would bring anybody out. You
the siren girls. Send chills through a body. What your name again?

Beulah
Beulah. I thank ye. I'm glad you mountain people come play with
us. You ain't half bad. Guards had us scared you'd hang us up if you
caught us out.

Elizabeth
Guards. Pshaw! You just like us, girl. Just want a free chance in the
world, and the way you sing and your feller plays, well, glory hallelujah,
you ought to be out singing to the world.

Jimmy
We shore appreciate your kindness. Come on, Beulah. We gotta get
you back to the stockade.

Isabella
You take care. I'll keep putting in a good word to Wilson for you
two. Let's go folks, we gotta a couple miles to cover. Get home fore
midnight.

Joseph
Sure is a strange world. I could of been with Bones on the chain
gang, or worse.

Elizabeth
But you had the courage to run away. Sometimes it takes more
courage to run than to stay, right Ben?

Ben
Yes, Elizabeth.

Isabella
Be careful, Ben talk you head off if you get him started.

Joseph
Yeah, he just said two words. He just getting warmed up. Speaking
of getting warmed up, we been walking for awhile now. Maybe stop
and take a sip. Warm us up a little bit, right, Ben?

Ben
Yes.

Isabella
See, you getting him started.

Ben
You go on ragging me. Me and fiddle might stay home next time
and talk to Dog and the stars all night.

Elizabeth
That was the longest sentence I ever heard him speak. Now leave
him alone and pass that jar over here.

Joseph
See that star up there high in the sky. It kind of red. That's Mars,
right, Ben?

Ben
Yep.

Joseph
Me and Ben knows the sky. When you live by yourself, you get a
long time to study the sky, and it studies you back. That's one of the
benefits.

Elizabeth
You been hitting the moonshine a little heavy ain't ya, Joseph?
Getting philosophical on us. Ariella, Andrew still off preaching? I can
see the cabin, and they ain't no lights.

Isabella
Yeah, he be gone for a couple more days.

Elizabeth
Well, here comes your hound dog, so I guess you be okay. I shore
had a lovely time. Let's have one more swig for good night and I'm
going to walk Joseph over to his place. He's a bit unsteady and don't
want him falling down any ravines and hurting his banjo. Trip over
something looking at Mars.

Joseph
One more swig I might just sprout wings and fly over there. You
people be safe. Ben, be careful on the trail up to your place. That trail
mighty slickery and dark. Well, good night, darlings.

Isabella
Thank ye for coming tonight, Ben. It was wonderful. Your fiddling
made the night.

Ben
Lotta people made this a good night, and it's me that ought to
thank you.

Isabella
Lizabeth right, that a mighty steep trail home. You're welcome to
stay here. Andrew's gone. We can stay up and talk or something. You
notice I kept the jar on that last go around. Ain't much in it, but that's
okay.

Ben
Stay here? Stay with you?

Isabella
Yes, don't sound so scared. I won't bite you, at least not until we
have another drink or two.

Ben
Well. That would be right nice, I believe. Right nice.

CHAPTER 43

A Little Bird Told Me

Beulah
It's been a right nice spring since the parties started back. That creek water still just as cold. Here, take this with you today. Listen to those birds.

Jimmy
They singing cause they in love, and they know we in love. Big difference is they free and we ain't.

Beulah
You think birds fall in love like people.

Jimmy
No, not like people, better than people.

Beulah
How you know?

Jimmy
A little bird told me. How you know they don't?

Beulah

I don't know that's why I'm asking. Go on. You better get going. They can't be blowing up any tunnels if you ain't there.

Jimmy

I got something to ask you, Beulah. Since me and you been together a few months.

Beulah

We ain't been together. We been sneaking and shacking up ever now and then.

Jimmy

You know what I mean. I love you and you love me, and I been thinking.

Beulah

You want to marry me.

Jimmy

How'd you know?

Beulah

A little bird told me.

Jimmy

You funny. Beulah, you done spoiled my proposal.

Beulah

I'm sorry. Start over. You gonna get down on your knees. You got a ring?

Jimmy
Yep. Beulah, will you marry me? Here's the ring. I made it in the rail
yard. Made out a same stuff that carries the charge--mica, and feldspar,
and I found a ruby.

Beulah
In that case, yes, cause it's all likely to blow up on us.

Jimmy
What you mean?

Beulah
You know well as me, they ain't gonna let two convicts get married.
Where we gonna have the wedding? In our boxcar?

Starlight
I'll marry ye.

Jimmy
What? What the hell? Starlight, We didn't see you up in that tree.
You not in your usual place.

Starlight
Leaves coming in. I went up higher. Better view of the morning
stars. I'll marry you. I've been ordained. A little bird told me.

Jimmy
Well, you and your little bird better keep your mouth shut. Now
you come down and go with me, or you gonna get in trouble. Guards
already watching you pretty close because how crazy you been acting.

Starlight
No crazier than usual.

Jimmy

Well, no, not to us, but the boss and the guards started noticing.
Beulah, you need to get Starlight a job down here in the kitchen.

Beulah

Maybe if we talk to Ariella. She got some pull with the boss. . . So
we engaged?

Jimmy

Yes. We are, and look that ring fit real nice.

****

Starlight

My grannydaddy said when he was on the slave ship, my grannymomma got sick and died and a sailor threw her off the ship, but before
she hit the water, she turned into a bird, an albatross, and flew off and
followed that ship, and every dead slave they threw off turned into an
albatross.

Bones

Sounds like he was a good storyteller, like me. Did I tell ya the one?

Starlight

And those Albatrosses followed that ship until it got in sight of
land. One of the white men shot my grannymomma, the Albatross,
and so she died twice. Do we have to die twice? Is that why they chain
us together? Fraid we gonna fly away?

Bones

Ask the crows next time. They like to talk. Now get your head
down. Jimmy bout to light that fuse and you gettin ready to die once if
you don't get down.

Starlight

Come on, Bones. I'm gonna climb up this tree, and Albatross them.

Bones

You ain't. You get down fore I knock you over the head with this shovel.

Starlight

I can't hear nothin. Man, they messin with stuff they oughtn't be messin with.

Bones

Come on, grab your shovel, we gotta start diggin out the rock from the tunnel. I wish we could fly away.

Starlight

I ain't cut out for all this diggin and haulin. You ever see a bird dig a hole?

Bones

You gotta stop talkin or the boss gonna be after us. Now get your little bird legs movin.

Starlight

Bones! I can't see ya for the dust and smoke. You in here, Bones? I can't breathe. I'm inside the belly of a whale.

Bones

I'm right here. It'll clear in a minute. Just hang on to me, Starlight.

Starlight

I'm swallowed up. Belly of a whale. Died twice. I can't breath. Albatross me.

Bones
It's okay, Starlight. I can see ya now. See me. We gotta start digging.
It alright. I'm here. Look! Here's the other men. Start the song. Start
the chant. That's what you're good at. Singing the tunnel. Singin like a
bird.

Starlight
"Run, mourner, run, bright angels above."

Bones
Look out! Run Starlight! the wall giving in. Cave in! Holler loud!
Cave in and run like hell. Run Starlight, out this way! Toward the light!
Toward the light!

CHAPTER 44

A Secret Plan

Elizabeth

Land's sake, I ain't been with a man since my Calvin went off to the war and got'em self killed. We were young and I didn't like it all that much. Calvin could be kinda mean about it. Kind of turned him into a different animal, but you, Joseph, you real gentle.

Joseph

It like playing music, I reckon. I didn't know much about it neither, but I saw what my mama, Kadella, went through. Having babies, and having to sleep with a white man like John Carson whether she wanted to or not. Having his baby, but she loved those babies just like she loved me, despite it all. It taught me to respect a woman. You a good woman, Lizabeth. Maybe we ought to get married.

Elizabeth

Say what, Joseph Carson? You just a plain spoken man, ain't ya. Is that a proposal?

Joseph

Yes, a proposal by a plain spoken man. We ain't no spring chickens, and we been friends a long time.

Elizabeth
Well, I reckon I'll think on it for a day or two. Build up a little suspense. A girl no matter how old wants it to be a smidgen romantic. Did you hear what Ariella was talking bout last night at the shindig? Well, we was walking back up the mountain and she said that Jimmy and Beulah was engaged and want to get hitched.

Joseph
I did, yes, but they can't cause they convicts doing time, but they love each other, and Ariella has a plan to get Andrew to marry them at one of the parties. Have a secret wedding after the singing's done. Nothing for certain right now. Ariella going to work on Wilson a little bit. See if she can get him to let Beulah and Jimmy kind of slip away.

Elizabeth
Sounds like a tall order there. Wilson a hard man, I hear.

Joseph
Well, if anybody can soften him up it be Ariella.

Elizabeth
You right about that.

Joseph
I thought maybe then if Andrew marrying one couple he might just as well marry two. That's pretty romantic, I'd say. We be providing cover for Beulah and Jimmy too, but I do want you to think on it a day or two.

Elizabeth
Well now, Joseph, that changes things a might. Might not have to think about it that long.

****

Wilson
Ariella Isabella, I'm quite impressed with the work you've done here. You're a quick learner, and, of course, everybody loves you. I've got some friends in Raleigh. After we finish this road, I'll be able to get you a job in the city. Get you outta here like you want. Get you some more school. You'll be on your way. A whole new life away from these hillbillies.

Isabella
I'd like that. I hear you gotta bunch of new convicts coming in.

Wilson
One hundred and fifty. They arrive on the train in two weeks, so we gotta get the new barracks finished. The mudcut slowed us down considerable. We are a couple months behind. The dysentery outbreak didn't help either. Had to bring that doctor back in. Money's really tight. I'll need your help with the books and paperwork.

Isabella
You know the two convicts. Jimmy and Beulah, the ones that help make music on Saturday nights?

Wilson
I know Jimmy, he's a right smart negro, helps us set the nitro-glycerin mix and the charges. I ain't familiar with the girl.

Isabella
The girl a good worker. Smart too. Sings like an angel. We sing together.

Wilson
That so, I've seen her, but it's hard to hear from my office. I watch, but I think it's good for me not to mix too much with the convicts.

Isabella
Well, those two are sweet on each other.

Wilson
So ain't nothing new there. I know what goes on in the woods.
Guards keep me posted. Long as they do their work. I don't see no
harm in it.

Isabella
I don't mean like that. You said yourself Jimmy's smart. They're
civilized. They're in love. They want to get married, and I said I might
try to help them.

Wilson
There's no convict weddings here. When this work is done in a year
or two., They go back to prison to do their time.

Isabella
They still could be married. They just young kids. They didn't do
nothing. Just got arrested cause they black, and at the wrong place at
the wrong time.

Wilson
You shouldn't said you'd help them. Can't get married here. It isn't
legal. So don't you be getting on your high horse about them being
innocent. That's what they all say. You've been listening to your father
too much. Abolitionist do-gooder.

Isabella
I ain't on no high horse. Just trying to figure out right and wrong in
the world you live in. You always saying they ain't no harm in it. Ain't
no harm in them getting married. They people James, they're not your
mules.

Wilson

Good thing about mules is they don't want to get married. I told
you it's not legal, so let that be the end of it.

Isabella

It legal for one of your guards to take advantage of some the convict
girls in the woods? Is it legal for em to shoot down a man for no
reason? Is it legal for people to have to work and not get paid a dime? If
you got money, it might be legal, but you know as well as me, it ain't
right.

Wilson

Maybe you're not as quick a learner as I thought. Better learn the
ways of the world before you get neck deep in it. I'm not listening to no
preaching from a mountain child. The world is what it is. I didn't
make it. I got a job to do and I do it. So young lady I have to prepare
the camp for 150 more convicts. Innocent or guilty, it is not for me to
say. I'll feed them and house them. In a world where most the white
boys got killed in a war and most the negroes are in prison, it's not my
decision and that's the world we live in. Not the fantasy fairy world of
Ariella Isabella.

****

Starlight

Jimmy and Beulah going to get married. Shh! Don't tell nobody.
Ain't nobody suppose to know. A little bird told me. It Sunday morning and I'm up in my church tree. We had a party last night and the
mountain folk come down and it was quite the soiree. But I heard em
whispering. Plotting something. Oh yeah. I'm what they call clairvoy-
ant. I had a boyfriend once, his name was Clair Voyant. He was a
dancer in New Orleans. He could tell the future and was into voodoo
and all that. He taught me a lot. He taught me to talk to the birds and
how to read the future in the clouds and such. Everything a little

cloudy now. All I can say is--some good things gonna happen, and some bad thing gonna happen too.

****

Elizabeth
Andrew, I have a request to make ye. It not an easy request.

Andrew
Yes. Lizabeth, What is it?

Elizabeth
Well, you know Joseph and I been friends a long time now. Nigh on a couple years after Calvin got himself killed, and well, he asked me to marry him t'other day, or I asked him, I ain't sure which, and we wanted you to be the one to marry us.

Andrew
Why that's wonderful news. Isn't a difficult request at all? I'll be happy too.

Eliz
Well, that ain't the end of the request.

Andrew
No, then what else?

Elizabeth
Well, you know the two young convicts we go sing with. Well, Ariella tells us they sweet on each other, and they want to get married, but Wilson told her they can't cause they convicts.

Andrew
Yes, what's that got to do with me?

Elizabeth

Well, Joseph and me thought since you going to marry us. We could get married before one of the parties at the camp, and you could marry them too, you know, in secret.

Andrew

What! That does complicate things doesn't it. I don't really want to do anything against Wilson. It'd get us all in trouble, especially Ariella.

Elizabeth

He won't find it out. We got a plan.

Andrew

I was afraid of that.

Elizabeth

In a couple weeks they bringing in a couple hundred more convicts. We figure there's a week before they get here. We'll go down to the singing like we been doing. There's a grove off on the other side of Mill Creek, not anybody know about. You'll marry Joseph and me, and at the same time, Jimmy and Beulah. You know they didn't do nothing to deserve to be in prison like they are. Treated like animals.

Andrew

Well, let me think about that. I need to talk to Ariella. I suspect this is mostly her doing. She thinks she's Cupid, but I guess I could.

Elizabeth

Well, and there one more thing.

Andrew

One more? What pray tell?

Elizabeth

Once they married, we need to get em out of the camp. Cause once they done with the road, they'll send em back to prison, so we need to help them escape. Once they married and the party over, we'll bring em back here. Next day Sunday, so nobody keeping up with anybody else, and besides Wilson will be so busy with the new convicts coming. They can stay at Lost Cove since Joseph will be at my cabin. Then, we figure, you can go off on a preaching trip, and sneak them over past Asheville. I have a cousin in Marshall who can hide them. We got it all figured out.

Andrew

Except for the part that says I'll get involved in this shady enterprise.

Elizabeth

Well, that's why I'm asking now.

Andrew

How many laws we breaking here?

Elizabeth

Oh, who's countin? If you break one you might as well keep going.

Andrew

I'd say helping convicts escape is a pretty serious crime. If Ariella already talked to Wilson they'll know we helped them, it'll be the first place they look.

Elizabeth

They'll be long gone time they figure out they're missing. They'll look a little bit, but they so busy finishing that tunnel, and getting it ready. They ain't gonna worry bout no two convicts for long. Then the road be finished and they'll go back to Raleigh. We can even bring em back here after a year or so. Hate to break up a good band.

Andrew
That's true, even though we might all be in jail.

Elizabeth
P'shaw. We ain't going to jail.

Andrew
I'll think on it. I'll talk to Ariella and Joseph bout all this. Seems a bit half cocked and fantastic to me, but congratulations to you and Joseph. I'm happy for you.

CHAPTER 45

Ariella is a Marvel

Ariella
(*Mountain song on dulcimer*)
"Come all you fair and tender ladies."

Ben
You gettin the hang of that dulcimer pretty quick. I figured you
would.

Ariella
It's beautiful. It almost plays itself. You got good hands for making
delicate things. Good hands, and a good kisser too.

Ben
You got something you want me to do. You sweet talking me pretty
good here.

Ariella
Why, Ben. I'm just complimenting my sweet feller, but there is
something you can do. I have a plan.

Ben
Uh oh, I was afraid of that.

Ariella
You ain't got to do much. I just need to tell it so I keep it straight in my head. You know, Jimmy and Buella want to get married.

Ben
No, I didn't know that.

Ariella
But Wilson said no. I tried to reason with him but if the numbers don't line up in his head, or something seems wrong, he's right hard to convince. So he say it's not legal and he won't stand for it.

Ben
And so?

Ariella
Well, me, Joseph and Elizabeth come up with a plan. You know, Joseph and Elizabeth, they gonna get married.

Ben
I didn't know that.

Ariella
Well, they are, and so Elizabeth talking to Andrew bout marrying them down at the camp before one of the parties, and marrying Jimmy and Beulah at the same time, you know, in secret.

Ben
Lotta people getting married, maybe you and me ought get married too. . . Don't look at me like that. I'm joking.

Ariella

Don't you ever joke bout that, Ben. You the best man I know and
I'm considerable fond of you.

Ben

Ariella Isabella, I'm too old fer you. We ain't talked about it before,
but you ain't marrying no old man like me.

Ariella

You ain't no old man, and girls round here marry much older men
than you. But you done got me off the subject and flustered. Now
listen, after Andrew marries them, then we sing and party, and afterwards we take em with us and hide em for a day or two, and then
Andrew sneaks them in his wagon over to Marshall. Elizabeth got a
cousin over there gonna hide em.

Ben

Well, Ariella, you shore make life interesting, but where do I come
in? What do I have to do?

Ariella

You just play your heart out on that fiddle, and afterwards help me
get em up the mountain and away the next day. Then, for a few days
I'm going to collapse at your place, in your arms, and you gonna take
care of me fore I have to go back to work and face Wilson. You think
you can handle that.

Ben

Playing my heart out on the fiddle and taking care of you. Taking
care of you might be a bit of challenge, but I think I'm up to it.

****

Jimmy

So it's almost time. It be just a few days. You still wanna marry me
and run away.

Beulah

Can't get married if we don't run, I reckon. You scared?

Jimmy

I reckon. Little bit. Lots has to go right for us to get away, but I love
ya and can't stay a convict. We ain't convicts. We deserve to be free.

Beulah

That's right, and that be the last words of a lot people like you and
me, but if these mountain folks willing to put their lives at risk for us. I
trust em.

Jimmy

I trust em too. They hired some new guards t'other day since they
bringing in a couple hundred more convicts. I don't like the looks of
the new guards. Some of em just kids, 17 or 18. They have a certain
mean look about em. You been around em awhile and you learn pretty
fast which ones you can trust a little bit or talk to a little bit, and which
ones just as soon shoot you as look at you.

Beulah

You working up at the tunnel tomorrow?

Jimmy

Yep, setting charges and blowing things up.

Beulah

You just be careful. Don't go and get yourself killed fore we get
married. Ariella showed me this grove yesterday fore the party. She said

this be a good place to marry us. A little clearing on the other side of the creek away from everything but not too far away. She call it a fairy place.

Jimmy
Now we here, and by next Saturday we be married just like a fairy story. Get Bones to make a Brother Rabbit tale for us.

Beulah
Brother Rabbit meets Sister Fairy. What's it gonna be like to be married? Not be made to work for nuthin, but our own selves.

Jimmy
Elizabeth say she know a cousin off in some other mountains round here going to set us up in a little cabin. Hide us for a while, but we be free to have some chickens and maybe a cow and a goat. Raise us some beans.

(*singing softly*)
"Cornbread and butterbeans and you across the table.
Making love and eating beans as long as we are able."

Beulah
Sounds too good to be true. I hope it ain't.

Jimmy
It ain't. We just gotta follow Ariella and do what she tell us. She a marvel, and it must not be an accident that we find her, or she find us. Wilson be so busy this week with the new convicts and building the new tunnel, and it a long one this time. The longest yet. We'll be bedding down far away from here time he knows us gone.

Beulah
My husband. I do like the sound of that.

CHAPTER 46

Some Good Things and Some Bad Things

Starlight

When I was a kid in New Orleans, I knew a trumpet player who was getting married and they was a procession, a parade coming down the street making all kinds of music and commotion, and I climbed up one of those new light poles to get a better view and that was the first time I climb up and see the world like I suppose to see it. Well, now that wedding pass by and the music and the singing. It was a sight to behold and I being so little and poor. I thought maybe that's the way that life was suppose to be. Celebrating by being alive. But I got a little older and because people told me I wasn't anything. I was a nothin. I wasn't a boy or a girl and maybe they just kill me and rid the world of my nothing kind. Well, it made me climb a little higher, and I started finding big old oak and cypress trees to climb and draping myself with Spanish Moss. I didn't know what they mean when they call me a nothing. I was just who I was. I was just bein like those stars and planets I became friends with. They ain't none of those stars making fun of Mars cause he red. Then, a while later, I up in a tree on Bourbon Street and here come another wedding, but it coming a little slower and the music, it be a little more mournful. And I call down to a boy and ask him who was getting married, and he look up at me like I'm some strange bird, and he say, "What you asking? It ain't no wedding but a funeral procession." And I ask him who died?" He tell me it Biggs, the best trumpet player in Storyville, and it the same man who was getting married a few years back when I learned to climb up on the world. I say but they celebrating. He say, yeah. We celebrating his life and sending him off to the angel, Gabriel, and a new band. I think it like he marrying death in a way, but I don't say it out loud. I just watch that procession go by, and wonder what kind of life this is.

Guard

Hey, you up there! What you doing up in that tree?

Starlight

I'm celebrating life.

Guard

You what? You get down right now and get back to the stockade.
You ain't suppose to be out here.

Starlight

Who you? You one of the new guards they talking bout?

Guard

Yep, I reckon I am. Now you get down.

Starlight

You just a kid. How old are you?

Guard

Seventeen and I'm old enough to kill me a convict.

Starlight

You see that star up there. It a million years old. It's its birthday.

Guard
You that crazy boy they was telling me about. You that queer boy. I have a mind to shoot you out that tree right now.

Starlight
Now why you want to do that. A young boy like you. The world already made you that mean? I might be the bestest friend you ever had. I might be like that star up there. Maybe the stars just dead people's soul that got killed by meanness and hatefulness.

Guard
I'm going to count to three, and you better come down.

Starlight
Think big. Count to ten. I bet you can't. Can't read neither, I bet. You count to ten. I'll come down. I's coming down anyway.

Guard
You smart mouth son of a bitch, my Winchester rifle will count to ten for ya. Now you march on back to the stockade where you suppose to be.

Starlight
You a bad, bad man with that rifle. Gonna take you a long way down. Down into the ground, and then down into hell. Happy birthday, star. I'm your starlight.

Guard
Hey. you walking the wrong way, stockade back this way.

Starlight
I'm walking the way I always walk. Happy birthday to you. A million years old.

Guard
Stop!

Starlight
I just singing. I ain't hurting nobody. You new here. You don't
know your way round yet. Here, let me give you a guided tour.

Guard
You trying to escape. You stop now.

Starlight
The last sound I remember was the pop of that rifle and I felt the
bullet go in my back and push me forward like it was telling me to run
faster. The last thing I saw was an Albatross circling above me. The last
thing I smelled was the smell of the cedar bark on my fingers. The last
thing I touched was the ground coming up to meet me. Then I
dreamed that Albatross, and a hundred other birds came and carried
me away. The last thing I thought was, happy birthday. A million years.

****

Jimmy
Bones! You seen Starlight? His bunk empty.

Bones
He gets up fore dawn sometimes to sit in his tree.

Jimmy
I just been out there he ain't in any of his trees.

Bones
Maybe he found a new one. Go ask Beulah, she real close with him
lately. Got'em that job in the kitchen, maybe he's with her.

Jimmy

I ain't got time right now. We headed up to explode some of that
tunnel. You coming too.

Bones

I's coming too, but I can run by the kitchen first on my way. Maybe
Beulah give me a biscuit or something.

Beulah

No, I ain't seen him since yesterday right after sundown. He up in
his tree talking crazier than usual. Talking bout some birthday star, or
something. I hope he didn't have a crack up and try to run away or
somethin crazy.

Bones

We ain't seen him this morning. Jimmy's had to go up to the big
tunnel they're blasting and I'm on my way there right now.

Beulah

He should be here by now helping me. You check his tree.

Bones

Jimmy did.

Beulah

I'll ask around. See if Ariella heard anything.

****

Ariella

Morning, Mr. Wilson, those new convicts coming tomorrow? You
want me to do some of the paper work on those new men you hired.

Wilson
You could do that later. What you know bout those Foxe boys we
hired as guards?

Ariella
Not much to know. Never had much truck with their family. They
claim to be twins, but they ain't never saw a lie they didn't like, from
what I hear. Their daddy was in the war. Turned him crazy mean, and
seems he passed that on to his boys. People generally knew to stay away
from their place which was easy to do cause they live purty far back in
the hollar. Why you want to know?

Wilson
Last night one of'em. Frick or Frack or Jeb or Reb, whatever their
names are, killed one of the convicts. Claimed he was trying to escape,
but I ain't convinced. I got both down by the stockade. We need'em as
guards. I can't fire them, but I can't have'em just shooting convicts for
the fun of it. Course the boy they shot wasn't good for much.

Ariella
You'll have to train some of the meanness out of'em. Dock their pay
for a week. Greedy is in their bag of hatefulness too. They like the seven
dwarves, Meany, Greedy, Dummy, that's what they ought be named.
Who was it they shot?

Wilson
You know, that crazy one, you talked me into letting him help in the
kitchen cause he was no good up on the road. Acted more like a
woman than a man. Went by some fairy name or something, so no
great loss there. Still I can't have the guards be so trigger happy.

Ariella
Oh no, not Starlight. Please no. Wouldn't hurt a firefly. Where is
he?

Wilson
We got his body down by the creek. Going to bury him later. Maybe
make that boy dig his grave. Teach him a lesson.

Ariella
Oh no, Starlight was part of the band.

Wilson
Look, Ariella. I'm running no summer camp here. I got a road to
build. We had twelve die last month of the dysentery. Had to bring a
doctor in. We have no money to hire anyone else. I can't worry bout
your band.

Ariella
Where's his body? Me and Jimmy take care of burying him.

Wilson
His body laid out down by the creek.

Ariella
Tomorrow Saturday. We'll bury him then.

Wilson
Bury him up in that tree for all I care. I got enough on my mind as it
is. Take care of that paper work first. I have to go up the tunnel where
they finishing the new stockade.

****

Beulah
You find him, Ariella?

Ariella

Starlight dead, Beulah. Some new guard shot him. Said he was trying to escape.

Beulah

That ridiculous. Starlight would never try to escape.

Ariella

No, I spect it was cold blooded murder. Just wanted to kill somebody. Make'em feel like a man. Nothing to be done bout it though. I talked to Wilson. He got other fish to fry so he don't care. I told'em we'd bury him.

Beulah

Poor lost soul, Starlight. World don't deserve sweet souls like that anyway. He was going to play his thumb piano at the wedding tomorrow. Now we got a funeral and two weddings on the same day.

Ariella

Yep. What's done is done. But we can get you and Jimmy out of this hellhole. I use to respect Wilson. You know, all his single-mindedness. His success. Now I see it's just a blindness. A blindness of purpose. Denying half the world so you can have the other half, but we gotta a lot to do fore tomorrow. We'll get the band to bury Starlight tomorrow afternoon, I figure, out there, near his trees. His trees look after him now.

Beulah

God Bless him. Yes, just before dark. Jimmy and me will meet you all in that grove you showed us how to get to. All of you will be there already, and preacher Andrew will marry us.

Ariella
Then what?

Beulah
Then we go sing and party just like we always do, but this time we'll
have a secret to celebrate.

Ariella
And?

Beulah
What? Oh yeah, we need to lay off the moonshine a little bit. Not
altogether mind ya, since we be celebrating, but not drink too much
cause we have a long road ahead of us.

Ariella
Then when the party break up, and convicts break up into small
groups before they go back to the stockade. You and Jimmy will go
with us back up the mountain. We got a cabin for you to stay in. Then
on Monday, Andrew will hide you in his wagon and he'll take you off
on the other side of Asheville. Elizabeth's cousin says she will hide you
up there. It way back on the other side of the world.

****

CHAPTER 47

Two Weddings and a Funeral

Bones
I'm all fer making a decent send off fer our friend, but digging six feet round these roots is a chore, and digging ain't somethin I'm too fond of on a Saturday afternoon after digging already fer a half day.

Jimmy
Stop ya whining, we almost there. We wanted Starlight to rest among his trees. Those trees talk to him and cradle him now fer all eternity. He knew how to talk to trees and birds better than he could with humans.

Bones
Look that crow up there brought some of his buddies. They say crows are awfully smart birds. I know a story bout ol' Brother Crow. . .

Beulah
Save that fer later, Bones. We gotta do this respectful, and we ain't got much time. Sun bout down now.

Bones
Crows keeping their distance, but these cardinals and mockingbirds right here in the tree. I guess they come to pay their respects. Sing us your song, mockingbird, that song you stole from me.

Jimmy
I reckon that good. Here, Starlight, you a sweet soul, too sweet fer this place. Laying you under this tree in your tattered blanket and your kalimba. I guess them words enough.

Bones
Amen, I'll stay and cover him up, and then I'll go get the instruments ready and cause a general ruckus while you two get hitched. Bless you children, I sure wish I could come with ya, but I'm old and ain't my place. You children take care and be careful. I be tellin stories bout you when all this mess is over, and this road finished.

Beulah
Come on, Jimmy, we gotta skedaddle. They be waiting. I bet Elizabeth and Joseph beside themselves with worry. Don't want to be late fer our own wedding.

Jimmy
We gonna miss ya, Bones. You keep playing banjo and telling your stories. Next time you see us we'll be husband and wife.

****

Andrew
Where are they? We gotta bout thirty minutes of light left. It ain't much time to marry em.

Joseph
Going into marriage in the dark probably ain't the right way to go.
Wouldn't you say Elizabeth?

Elizabeth
Joseph Carson, if you say one more joke bout this wedding, I might
just call it off right here.

Joseph
Don't do that. I always joke when I'm nervous, and I'm double
nervous. One, for getting married and another, for those two children
we helping escape.

Elizabeth
You got the ring?

Joseph
Right here in my pocket, or some pocket, or maybe I put it in my
shoe.

Elizabeth
I'm going to give you something to be nervous about here in a
minute. That's my momma's ring. I wonder what she think of me
getting married out here in the woods.

Andrew
She would think you're good people for doing this.

Ariella
Here they come. Thank goodness. Hello, you two. Come on catch
your breath, and line up here behind Elizabeth and Joseph. We got no
time to waste here.

Jimmy
We had to bury Starlight. We run all the way here.

Ariella
God bless his soul. May he rest in peace. Funeral and two weddings
in the same day, same hour really. Now we gotta marry you two.

Ben
You two glowing you're so purty.

Beulah
We glowing cause we run a mile down this trail.

Ben
You and Elizabeth don't look too bad yourselves.

Elizabeth
You men a barrel of laughs. Be careful Benjamin, or I'll bonk you
with Joseph's banjo here.

Ariella
Everybody just hush now. You ready, Andrew.

Andrew
Friends, we are gathered here today to wed in holy matrimony these
four people.

Ben
Not all of them together mind ya.

Ariella
Shush, Ben.

Andrew
You, Beulah, whatever yer last name is.

Beulah
Beulah Rose.

Andrew
Beulah Rose and Jimmy Johnson and Elizabeth Moore and Joseph
Carson.

****

Ariella
"In the gloaming. . ."

It was sure a purty wedding in the woods. Andrew said it reminded
him of Shakespeare and the forest of Arden, or something like that. It
was definitely different.

Elizabeth
Ben, you need to get going back up there to the stockade.

Ariella
Yes. Bones supposed to be setting up the music, and getting things
ready. I'll go too. I gotta talk to Wilson bout some work stuff, and kind
of feel things out. Make sure he so busy he ain't gonna worry bout two
convicts. Congratulations, you lovebirds. See ya at the party.

Beulah
We married now, Jimmy. Me and you, husband and wife.

Jimmy
It something ain't it. Who'd thunk it?

Elizabeth
Who'd a thunk it, indeed. And you all gonna have a nice long life.
My cousin gonna take care of ya, and get you all set up.

Beulah
We thank ye awful much for your kindness.

Joseph
You welcome. You deserve it. Now let's celebrate with a little drink.
Get the blood running and then go dance and sing.

Elizabeth
One drink. You hear me. We gotta pace ourselves cause we gotta a
long night ahead of us.

Joseph
You listen to that. Would you? Ain't been married fifteen minutes
and she already bossing me round. Trying to make a christian out of
me.

Elizabeth
You a funny man, Joseph. You must still be feeling nervous joking
like that. I might boss ya little bit, but I wouldn't try to make no
christian man out of ya. I ain't no fool.

Joseph
Here's to us. A long, happy life.

Jimmy
Cheers.

CHAPTER 48

Things Go Awry and the Nick of Time

Wilson

Ariella, there you are! Before the singing starts I need you to file these names and numbers for me for the new guards. The new bunch of convicts just getting settled, so this their first Saturday night, but we are keeping them in tonight before we turn them loose down here. They gotta work hard a whole week before they get to party. Learn how things work. Get mingled a little bit with experienced convicts.

Ariella

Okay, what'd you do with that guard killed Starlight?

Wilson

Put him under guard for a couple days. Give him a good talking to. Told him if it ever happened again I'd fire him.

Ariella

He killed a man. You make it sound like he got drunk or something. He killed somebody fer no reason.

Wilson
Don't start that with me tonight, Ariella. I'm run about ragged
here, and we're behind schedule, and we got a tunnel to finish this
week, and a trestle to build. I'm short on guards as it is. I put him with
his brother who seems more level-headed. They are up the mountain at
the stockade with the new convicts.

Ariella
Alright. I'll finish this, but I don't want to miss the singing.

****

Ben
Whoa! I am fiddled out. I ain't never fiddled that long. I was
supposed to fiddle, "Ae Fond Farewell" at the end while the party is
over and everybody is middling round talking and stuff, pairing off,
and such. Then while Ariella is getting Jimmy and Beulah away, I'm
supposed just to watch out nobody follows, and then come along
behind a little later. That's okay, I guess. That wasn't in the original
plan, but I can do it. I just have to play this lament, and keep my eyes
open. Most of the guards up at the tunnel stockade with the new
convicts. This is breaking up like it always do.

Elizabeth
Come on, children just cover up your heads. There, like that.

Joseph
Kind a walk in the middle of us til we get across the creek and the
trail narrows. We gotta good hour to walk, and then you'll be free.

Ariella
Moon's purty bright so keep your heads down. Just look down at
your feet walking.

Jimmy

Thank ye. That some party tonight. Singing and playing like I'm a
free man.

Beulah

It shore was. No more washing those big pots in that ol' cold creek,
or having those guards watch me bathe and talking and snickering.

Elizabeth

Nope, you're husband and wife now. We gotta a ways to go and we
gotta walk pretty close to that new camp and stockade. It best if we
don't chatter for a while. Just walk.

Andrew

We're a ways above the tunnel camp now. We're almost home free.

Joseph

That mean we can stop and have a little snort of moonshine in this
little clearing up here. I over paced myself, I believe, and it been a
couple hours since we toasted to the newlyweds.

Guard One

Halo there! What you people doing out here?

Guard Two

You taking a midnight stroll?

Elizabeth

I know you two boys. You the Foxe twins. What you doing up here?
We been down at Henry Station making music, and a little dancing.
We on our way home now.

Guard 1
We guards. Boss hired us a couple weeks ago. Who you got between you there? It wouldn't be you trying to help some niggers escape.

Guard 2
My Winchester here says you people might be up to no good.

Joseph
Naw! They free men like me. They're my cousins came to visit.

Guard 1
Step out, niggers. Let me see ya. Take off those hats and covers.

Guard 2
Let's see what freemen wear to a dance. Why you convicts. You trying to pull a fast one. You trying to escape ain't ya?

Jimmy
No sir. We free. Like Joseph here says.

Guard 1
Joseph one of ya too. He escape too. Just a long time ago. Never been caught's all. My daddy told us all bout you people.

Guard 2
And you with a white woman too. Maybe we shoot all of you.

Andrew
Please, men, we don't mean any harm. We're just walking home. These two are husband and wife. We're just taking them up to our cabin for the night. They're going to preaching with us tomorrow. Then we'll bring them back down. Jimmy here works the nitroglycerin with Wilson.

Ariella
Yes, he's like a trustee, and Beulah works for me, and I work for Wilson. He'll be mighty upset if he finds out you stopped us this way.

Guard 2
Well, well, if it ain't the fancy preacher man we hear bout, and his pretty Mexican whore.

Guard 1
Come here, Mexican whore. I might want a little piece of you myself. Let's kill the others.

Guard 2
Up here trying to escape. We told ya to stop but ya wouldn't. We'll shoot the white folks first. Ladies first. Let's see, I'm pointing my Winchester at the plump woman's head.

Andrew
The next sound I heard that broke their chatter was a pop, and the guard holding the Winchester suddenly lurched forward and landed face down. The back of his skull parted by a bullet.

Elizabeth
The other guard turned and the next sound I heard was another pop and the guard fell. His shirt turning red from the blood.

Ariella
And there stood Ben. The large pistol gripped in his hands. Looking as surprised as the rest of us.

Jimmy
They dead. You killed them.

Beulah
You saved our lives.

Ben
I suspect that wasn't part of the plan was it? I stayed behind at the
camp and was trying to catch up with ya before ya reach the mountain
trail. I heard em fore I saw em. So I snuck up real slow to the edge of
the clearing behind this tree. Those are two killers. I seen their likes
plenty.

Ariella
But the gun? I ain't never seen that pistol before.

Ben
Old civil war pistol. When I deserted I threw down my rifle, but I
kept my pistol for protection for the long journey. I had it put away,
but then I thought with what we're doing, helping Jimmy and Beulah.
I thought it might be good to bring it along just in case. I'm just glad it
fired. I won't sure. Sitting idle for that many years. I'm just glad I could
get close enough to'em. I only had three bullets.

Joseph
You saved us. . . But we can hero you later cause now what do we
do?

Andrew
First, we need to bury these two. Quick! Drag em off the trail, and
we'll bury them in the soft stuff by this creek. Joseph can come back in
a day or two. Bury them deeper, so no animals dig em up.

Joseph
I'll come back in the morning, in case, somebody comes looking for
em.

Elizabeth
Ain't nobody gonna come looking for these two. Their daddy,
maybe in a week or two.

Ariella
Wilson will be too busy to worry bout two guards he didn't trust
anyway. He'll think they just took off back home. Certainly won't
suspect we killed and buried them.

Ben
But when he misses Jimmy and Beulah, he'll suspect us right away
with helping them, won't he? I mean, you talked to him about letting
them marry. He'll come snoopin up here first.

Ariella
Yeah, maybe. Let me handle Wilson. I'll think of something, and by
then Jimmy and Beulah be on the other side of Asheville. But let's not
let these two worthless boys ruin your honeymoon. Let's get going.

Ben
Yeah, better enjoy it while you can. We might all be in prison fore
it's over.

****

Jimmy
Come here, wife. I got to carry you over the threshold of this cabin.
We married and we free.

Beulah
It's a mighty strange feeling, being free, but we gotta ways to go fore
we can stop running.

Jimmy
We made it this far. We'll make it. Now I'm gonna lay you on that ol bed over there.

Beulah
It's so late. We better get some sleep fore the long trip tomorrow.

Jimmy
What you talking bout sleepin for? It our honeymoon and it may only be a six hour honeymoon, but time gonna stop for us, and maybe, we ain't gonna go anywhere tomorrow. Tomorrow Sunday.

Beulah
I reckon you right husband, if time ever stop for folks it be on a Sunday.

Jimmy
That's right. I think we go with preacher Andrew on Monday morning, so stop the jabbering, woman, and kiss me.

****

Elizabeth
Well, Joseph. You my husband now. I don't know. We awful old. Can't teach an old dog new tricks.

Joseph
Pshaw, woman, young as ya feel. Course right now, I feel like a 102 after what happened tonight, but one more little shot of shine here and I'll be rejuvenated, and I'll show what an old dog can do.

Elizabeth
Listen at you. Making an old woman blush. . . I am scared, Joseph. Plan didn't quite work like we had figured. Everything else have to run smooth now.

Joseph
It will. I go down first thing in the morning and bury those boys so
deep in the ground, devil have a short trip up to claim em.

Elizabeth
That mighty hard diggin.

Joseph
Ben said he come help. He said I shot em. I'll help bury them.

Elizabeth
God bless him.

Joseph
It'll be fine. It's fated, I believe. They ain't no way that ol pistol of
his should a fired on the first try, and that was the only try he had. Now
here take a sip. I don't want to talk no more.

****

Ariella
Ever kill anybody before, Ben, in the war and all, or in a fight?

Ben
Nope, after I deserted I been to myself all these years and ain't ever
had a cause to kill anybody, til now.

Ariella
You saved us. It was courageous.

Ben
Did what I had to do. Didn't have time to think it out, so nothing
much to do with courage. Like any animal it was self-preservation.

Ariella
You kill many animals?

Ben
You know as well as I, you live up here ya gotta hunt to eat, but I do prefer fishin myself. Living alone, it less trouble. Joseph and Andrew slaughter a hog from time to time.

Ariella
It felt funny tonight. All our friends getting married. All that love in the air. I felt kind of left out.

Ben
Andrew was with us. He didn't get married.

Ariella
But Andrew was doing the marrying. Channeling all that love 'tween such good people. I just felt it, you know?

Ben
What you driving at Ariella Isabella? You ain't saying you think you and me ought to get hitched.

Ariella
Well, I ain't saying, but we doing everything else. We gonna raise a scandal if we ain't careful.

Ben
Twixt who? The squirrels and the possums gonna start gossiping?

Ariella
I was just thinking. We got somethin awful special 'tween us.

Ben

We do, by God, don't think I don't know we do, but we also got a passel of years tween us, and you said yourself you wanna go out and see what's out in the world, and you should, so let's not talk about getting married. I love ya more than I could ever put into words, and it's late and we've had a little bit to drink, and I killed two low down scoundrels, and now I just wanna kiss you, and lay down beside you, and that is the most heavenly thing there is. That's as close as we get.

The Last Tunnel

Wilson

Good morning, Ariella, I have to go up to the new tunnel. We'll be blasting more today, but I have some paperwork I need you do for me. Also, I have a couple questions, and some good news as well for you.

Ariella

Good morning, Mr. Wilson.

Wilson

It's Wednesday. We blast today and seems like nobody's seen Jimmy since Saturday night, and seems like the little negro girl you were talking about that sings with em is gone too. You wouldn't know anything bout that would you?

Ariella

Naw sir, been working here. Ain't seen em neither. They gone, you say?

Wilson

Yep, gone, and Jimmy one of the best workers I had. He was on the blasting crew. Him and Bones were the only convicts on that crew. Leaves me short-handed.

Ariella

You reckon they run off?

Wilson

I reckon they did, and I reckon somebody round here knows something who isn't talking. Anyway, I have to file a report and I want you to write it up. I have to send it to Raleigh when convicts escape, but I been thinking what we talked about some weeks ago. About them wanting to get married, and how they weren't really criminals. I believe I've come round to your side a little bit. Also, from a practical standpoint, we're going to be finished with this road in eight months or so, and we'll all be out of here. I don't have time to spend chasing after two convict lovebirds. I figure you got them hid somewhere deep in these mountains, and so let the mountains have them. I want to write up a report that says their names and when we first missed them, that would be today, and that they're presumed dead. Say we found one body along the French Broad, and we presume the other drowned too, so case closed.

Ariella

Mr. Wilson, I knew you were a good man. A by-the-book man, but a good man. I'll write that report up right away. You say you have some good news for me?

Wilson

Yes. I found you a job in Raleigh. It's a secretarial job with the state government. I've got some paperwork for you to fill out and send in. You'll probably start in a couple months, if you still want it.

Ariella

Well, things have changed for me here a mite. There's a lot bout this place I don't want to leave, but part of it is I'm just scared to try something that new. But I know I gotta take it for that reason. I need to see for myself what's out there in the world.

Wilson

Good. I'll send a letter with your paperwork in a week or so. I'll send some inquiries about a room in a boarding house near where you'll be working. You can take some classes at the college there.

Ariella

College? Never thought I'd hear my name and the word "college" in the same sentence. I guess I better start learnin how to speak proper.

Wilson

Well, maybe. Don't let them change you too much. You are a wonder.

Ariella

I thank ye for everything you've done for me.

Wilson

Well, I have to get up to the tunnel now. I'm short-handed and those two twin guards seem to have taken off too. Not enough action for them maybe.

Ariella

Yeah. Honest work and those boys just don't get along. Run off back home, I bet.

****

Convict
I sure wish I'd learned to play some musical instrument. The guitar,
or mouth harp, banjo or somethin.

Bones
What you talkin bout?

Convict
You niggers that play music. You get special treatment. Here you are
setting the charges on this nitro, blowing up the solid rock, while me
and the others have to then go and dig it with picks and shovels and
our bare hands sometimes. You music people got it easy.

Bones
Well, maybe so. It don't hurt, and it a mighty pleasin thing all to
itself. Could be I'm a might smarter than your average convict. I be like
Brother Rabbit.

Convict
Story man, smooth talker. You got it made, and where's Jimmy? He
too. He play and sing and then he run off with the prettiest gal in the
whole camp.

Bones
Well, maybe you should get a jaw's harp and learn it. It seem you
like to spin a tale yerself.

Convict
Convicts talking. They say something went on Saturday night.
Some secret ceremony or wedding, or somethin, and then they run off
into the mountains. Those mountain folks that play music with y'll,
they helped. I guess you music people stick together.

Bones
I reckon we do, and I'd appreciate it if you kept the gossiping to
yerself. . . Here comes boss.

Wilson
Bones get over here! Let's look at this rock face, and see where we
want to bore the holes.

Bones
Yes sir, comin!

Wilson
Bones, where do you think the holes ought to be drilled?

Bones
This rock face purty smooth. I think maybe six holes here, here, and
here.

Wilson
I think half as many will do well enough with this new mash.

Bones
Right, Cap'n. . . Here Billy, you hold the star drill, and I'll swing the
hammer. Turn the drill a smidgin after every time I hit it.

Wilson
Here. Take a breath. I'm going to pour some water in the hole to
cool down the bit.

Bones
That's two holes. One more to go.

Wilson

Here. Bones, let me show you this part since you ain't as familiar with it as Jimmy is, or Jimmy was. . .Here, I crimp the fuse into the percussion cap. Now the holes are ready, I funnel mash into them. Be careful not to drop it from a height. Gently tamp it with a stick to get it laid in hole tight, otherwise it loses compression in the blast. I put the cap well down in the center hole, then stab it with a stick. Daub all three holes using this stiff mud. Okay, now I'm going to light the fuse. Get ready. Run! Get behind that big rock.

Bones

What's happenin Cap'n?

Wilson

Not sure. I counted to thirty. Now I just finished going to sixty.

Bones

Time, yet.

Wilson

Just made it to a hundred. We're in trouble with this thing, gentle-men.

Bones

Why?

Wilson

That's the trouble. I don't know why.

Bones

Is it going to explode?

Wilson

I don't know. Something was wrong with that fuse, maybe. I meant
to get a detonation man, but nobody around here has ever used this
stuff before.

Bones

It's not worth it for you to risk your life. I could go see. I ain't scared
of it, and I ain't got a soul in the world.

Wilson

I just wish that nitroglycerin would blow and not have to inspect
the fuse. Do you know how to inspect?

Bones

Very carefully, Capt'n, I'd say. I'm going to take a look. The way I
got it figured, with time off for good behavior, I'll get out of prison
when I'm 110. The men are getting anxious.

Wilson

Okay, but careful, I'll stay here behind this rock and talk you
through it.

Bones

Hey, buddy, think playing music get you anywhere now.

Wilson

My dearest Louisa,
Those were the last words he said when suddenly it blew. Killed
Bones instantly. We buried him right there beside the entrance of the
tunnel. One convict run off and the other one just got killed. I'm going
to have to train a couple more convicts to help me with the nitro. Don't
worry, I'll be careful. I've got a man coming from Raleigh to help too.
We have one more tunnel to blow, but it's the big one up Swannanoa,

up near the top. Another seven or eight months and I'll be through with this God forsaken job, and I can come home to you dearest. It is lonely work here and I miss your sweet company.

Love,
Jim

****

Freedom

Andrew

Jimmy, you and Beulah can come out from that blanket now. We on a long lonely stretch a the turnpike, and it being Monday morning there won't be anyone much on the road. If I see somebody, I'll tell you to duck back down.

Jimmy

Yes sir, preacher Andrew.

Andrew

We have about a two hour ride to Asheville. Then we'll change roads up to Marshall. Take us most the of the day to get there. Congratulations, you're married now, and on your way to having a free life. Not without hardship mind you, but you're free.

Beulah

Yes sir, we know that, and sure appreciate your kindness. . . You never marry, preacher Andrew? You never have any children?

Andrew

No Beulah, I was married once. We were young. I was a seminary student in Boston. She was the daughter of a professor there. She was only seventeen. We should have waited, but you can't tell the young anything. We had the whole world. I took a parish out in the country.

She died of scarlet fever, and she was pregnant. Her parents never forgave me. I never forgave myself. We should have waited and took our time, but like I said, we were young and wanted to save the world. You cannot save the world. You can try to save little pieces of it and that's what I tried to do from then on.

Beulah
You never wanted to marry anyone else?

Andrew
I wasn't supposed to. I began to walk south. I didn't know where I was going. Walked a thousand miles and in walking I began to think of work and abolition. Big abolitionist movement in Boston. So on my walk, I met many people and I knew of a network of contacts that could help slaves escape. That's where I met Ariella and adopted her. I wandered into these mountains and it seemed like a good place to set up a station. Hidden, isolated, the people here split on slavery. Most are so poor they never owned a slave. They were slaves to this poor land themselves. I set up a small church, did the preaching circuit, met the Carson family down in Pleasant Gardens. That's how I met Joseph. That's how I helped him escape. Then the war came and ended. Barely knew there was a war way up here. Stoneman's cavalry came through, part of Sherman's outfit, so then slavery ended, at least, that brand of it.
I thought I was retired from helping slaves escape, but here we are. Now you two need to get down under that blanket for a bit. Round this next bend is a settlement and then Asheville, which we'll skirt by turning off the main turnpike, so we'll encounter some people soon.

Jimmy
That's a mighty interesting history. If it weren't for you, we wouldn't met Ariella, or Joseph, or Elizabeth, or you. It's just good to know they people in the world like you. Gives us some hope.

Andrew
Hope is a good thing. Hope will keep you going, but not if you get
caught, so keep down now.

****

Ben
I heared ya singing coming up the trail. Sound like a happy sound.

Ariella
Well, it both happy and sad, I reckon.

Ben
What's the happy part?

Ariella
Wilson not going to hunt after Jimmy and Buella. He had me write
up the report to send to Raleigh. Claims they drowned crossing the
French Broad and presumed dead.

Ben
That's very good news. He had a change of heart, I guess.

Ariella
Change of heart a good way to put it. I won't sure he had a heart,
but turns out he does after all.

Ben
Well, you seem to bring out the heart in everybody you meet. . .
Even me.

Ariella
Not everybody, and you already have the biggest heart I know.

Ben

I been thinkin a might bout what you said the other night bout us
gettin hitched.

Ariellla

Oh lands sake, that just crazy talk, I reckon. The moonshine talkin.

Ben

Yeah, I reckon.

Ariella

Oh don't get me wrong, Ben. I still think about it too. I love ya like
crazy, but you right. It ain't really practical.

Ben

Listen to you, talkin bout practical. You just help marry two
convicts, helped em escape, convinced your tight-assed boss to let it go.
Not exactly practical, I'd say.

Ariella

Don't ya want to know what the bad news is?

Ben

Well, good news and bad news ain't really like rice n' beans. I don't
much like to mix em up. Bad news is a flavor kinda overwhelms the
good, but I got a feelin you gonna serve it to me anyway.

Ariella

Wilson offered me that job in Raleigh. You know, the one we was
talkin bout. . . I took it.

Ben
Thought you said it was bad news. It good news, only part of it bad.

Ariella
I know, but it hard to think bout leavin you. Leavin here. I took it cause Andrew always told me if I wanted something it would scare me. Scare me into not doing it, and I'm scared to death, and I don't even know if I want to go.

Ben
You're going. End of story. Looks like a storm coming up.

CHAPTER 49

Epilogue

Ben

You know, Dog, it's been two years since the railroad finished. Now stead a hearing the dynamite going off, I hear the train whistle, and the chug of the train in the distance. I have to say it's a more pleasant sound than the nitroglycerin. Kind of peaceful in a way. Makes me glad I'm far distant from all that moving. The locomotive struggling to carry people who are always going somewhere, leaving from somewhere to get to somewhere else, but us. It makes me wonder bout Ariella. Wonder if she one of them moving? Moving up in the world. Finding her place in it. Seeing all sort of exotic places and things. She young. Hope she finding it out there. Me and you beyond all that. We both old dogs. Got this new dulcimer made of old wood though, and you old dog, older than me as far as a dog's life goes. Sleeping on the porch, dreaming of chasing rabbits. Yep, We right where we wanna be. Elizabeth, and Joseph, and Andrew growing old right along with us but the music keep our spirit young, I reckon.

THE END

Freddy Bradburn is a writer, songwriter, musician, and retired educator who lives with his wife in Pleasant Gardens, N.C., less than a mile from the Historic Carson House, and ten miles from where the railroad winds up the mountain from Old Fort toward Asheville. Freddy has had a musical about the Carson House and a Celtic folk opera produced by local community theater, and numerous recordings sitting in boxes in various places in his house. He also performs music with several Americana groups in the area. He also works with middle school students and recently wrote a musical based on his adaptations of Robert Frost's poems. He is currently writing a musical based on the 1929 textile strike in Marion.